UN$H

UN$HACKLED

HOW TO ESCAPE THE CHAINS
OF CONVENTIONAL WISDOM
THAT KEEP YOU POOR

ZACHARIAH B. PARRY, ESQ.

Distributed globally by Boss Media.
New York | Los Angeles | London | Sydney

Hardcover ISBN: 978-1-63337-423-2
Paperback ISBN: 978-1-63337-424-9
E-book ISBN: 978-1-63337-425-6
Library of Congress Control Number: 2020915398

Cover design by Jacob Parry, Laurence Noziak, and Zachariah B. Parry.

Manufactured and printed in the United States of America

To my wife, Amber, who was smart with money long before I was.

DISCLAIMER

HEY! ZACH PARRY HERE.

I hate to have to start my book off with a disclaimer, but I am a lawyer after all. The information I have compiled in this book is meant to provide you with some very valuable information related to money—how it works and grows and how others (especially the government) do their darndest to take it from you.

I have taken painstaking efforts to make sure everything in this book is well researched and accurate, but I can't guarantee that I didn't rely on misleading information or mess up a formula in my Excel calculations. The financial world is very complicated and constantly changing, and some of it varies state to state.

The information in this book is not intended to convey legal or financial advice specific to you or your circumstances. So before you rush off and change what you're doing based on something you've read in my book, please consult with a financial professional (but be careful whom you choose—there are a lot of charlatans out there), and make sure you are getting individualized advice based on your particular circumstances and goals.

If you have questions for me, you can reach me at this address: zach@fortunefirm.com.

TABLE OF CONTENTS

FOREWORD

THE GREATEST LIABILITY you will ever have in your life is the people you choose to listen to and to take advice from. This is one of the biggest barriers to true financial freedom because bad financial advice forms shackles just as restrictive as literal chains.

After billionaire Warren Buffett went on national television and announced to the entire world that he paid less in taxes than his secretary, people ran out of their houses in droves the next day. They rushed to their accountants and financial advisors looking to do the same thing Warren Buffett did.

But their advisors told them it couldn't be done. Some advisors said only gazillionaires could do it. Others said such a thing isn't legal. Others said it was just boastful fantasy. I could agree with these advisors, but then we'd all be wrong. Of course, when they said it couldn't be done, what they were really saying was that they just didn't know how to do it. They weren't getting paid enough to try to learn.

I have been blessed to sit at the feet of some of the richest and most successful businesspeople in the world, and I have come to learn one undeniable fact. Wealthy people just do things differently. Period! I saw an unfair playing field growing up. If you were born rich, married rich, or happen to know or meet wealthy people, then you were blessed to have access to the many amazing programs known to the haves but not the have-nots.

In a constant struggle to help consumers realize that they deserve more, we find that when it comes to success, people will often step on their opportunities. Due to conditioning, people have grown to believe somehow that they do not deserve to control or possess their own investable money. We accept it graciously, if not gratefully, when we are charged a penalty to access our own money. We accept the limits placed on what we can do with our own money and how we can invest it.

For some reason, we don't rebel at the fact that we can invest in other people's businesses but not our own. Not only do we tolerate stock market losses that on average since the 1800s occur to a magnitude of 43 percent every 9.875 years, but we put all of our retirement savings into it! And then during retirement, when we realize we don't have near what we thought we would have, we throw our hands up and blame the government.

Zachariah Parry truly stands as one of the finest litigating attorneys of our time. Having won almost every conceivable legal achievement award, Zach has stood at the forefront of the most advanced and affordable asset protection and tax strategies available anywhere in the world. This book is an amazing resource for anyone truly wanting to get into the minds of the ultrawealthy and learn what makes them tick, how they choose their investments and strategies, how they protect themselves from predators and creditors alike, and how they have amassed huge tax-free fortunes that have created a legacy. Sit back and relish the opportunity of learning from one of the greatest in his field while truly learning what the 1 percent do that the 99 percent do not. Get unshackled!

—Nick Fortune, LL.M., Ph.D.

INTRODUCTION

"A formal education will make you a living;
self-education will make you a fortune."
—JIM ROHN

I GREW UP KNOWING ALMOST NOTHING about money beyond the fact that if you had enough of it, you could trade it for just about anything you could want. As an eight-year-old kid, I didn't come by very much money, but when I did, I would walk the 1.7 miles down the street, across the canal, through a couple of strangers' yards, and past the cemetery to the corner drugstore to buy a pack of Topps Baseball Cards.

I didn't know if I liked baseball or not—I wouldn't start playing for another four years—but all my friends collected baseball cards, and conventional wisdom at the time was that baseball cards went up in value and, if you had enough, would eventually make you rich.

Plus, every pack contained a hard, dry stick of chewable sugar that made your baseball cards smell like bubble gum. After a couple of minutes of jaw-straining chomping, there was at least thirty or forty seconds that you could enjoy that ubiquitous childhood flavor before it got bland and too hard to chew.

I can remember being at my friend Jordan's house taking a break from playing *World Series Major League Baseball* on a Mattel Intellivision video game console long enough for him to show me a closetful of boxed baseball cards. He boasted that this would make him rich. I felt the same kind of awe that Huey, Dewey, and Louie must have felt when they first laid eyes on Scrooge McDuck's money bin. I figured Jordan was set for life.

When I was a teenager, I wasn't forward thinking enough with the money I earned from my weekly paper route to invest—most of my money went to CDs or *Star Wars* books. But I did buy baseball cards. I still remember feeling a kind of adult-level responsibility when I forked out thirty-four dollars to buy the 1994 Donruss and Score complete-set boxes of baseball cards (one was nineteen dollars, and one was fifteen dollars). Then they sat in my closet for years where I believed they were quietly working hard to provide for my future.

Twenty years later, as a hard-up-for-money second-year law student, I would learn the folly of getting investment advice from preteen baseball fans.

My wife, Amber, was preparing for a neighborhood-wide garage sale and saw my treasured baseball cards that had been sitting in our basement collecting dust (and supposedly value). I had kept them with me when my family moved from Southern California to Las Vegas when I was in high school, took them with me when I moved out of the house to go to college, kept them through my two-year stint as a missionary in El Salvador, and then lugged them across the country when I was in Illinois for law school.

Amber asked if she could sell them. I resisted and looked up their value to find justification for keeping them but was shocked to discover that they were almost worthless. I reluctantly gave her permission to sell them, though I insisted she try to get as much as she could.

Then at that garage sale in 2008, when the baseball cards were fourteen years old, my dear Amber sold them for six dollars each.

I was not happy when Amber told me the news, though it wasn't her fault they didn't fetch a good price. At the time of writing this book (in 2020), a 1994 Score complete set of 660 cards in near-mint to mint condition was worth fifteen dollars. So if I had wanted more than six dollars twelve years ago, I shouldn't have been selling them at a garage sale. Even if I had been able to find a buyer willing to pay top dollar, I was never going to get any more money than I paid for them anyway.

I can remember feeling a deep sense of loss reflecting on not only the devaluation of the thirty-four-dollar investment I had made in 1994, but also all the earnings I was supposed to be getting with the passage of time. I felt like I'd lost more than just twenty-two dollars (not accounting for inflation) because the future that those boxes promised for so many years would never come to pass.

I could have been spared this loss if the shop owner selling baseball cards had known enough to post a sign above those two boxes—"Complete-set Special: Spend thirty-four dollars today. Carry and store these two boxes for fourteen years, and then sell them for twelve dollars." I suppose that shop owner didn't know any better. If he had, he never would have opened a shop full of inventory destined to decrease in value.[1]

The lesson I learned then, which thankfully only cost me twenty-two dollars and the dissipation of some unrealistic dreams, was that conventional financial wisdom was a prison and that investing money as conventional wisdom dictates comes at a very real cost. Ultimately, it doesn't matter whether your investment advice comes from neighborhood boys, expensive commercials, published books, or TV pundits—bad advice is bad advice.

There are other lessons I have learned along the way that were more impactful (and came at a higher cost) than the one about baseball cards as investments. Although it's true that money can't buy happiness—in fact, money has nothing to do with the potential for happiness at all—wouldn't you rather be happy and rich than happy and poor?

I hope to be able to share with you some of the foibles of conventional wisdom and dispel common myths about how to invest, how to protect assets, how to save in taxes, and ultimately, how to unshackle yourself from the chains of conventional financial "wisdom" that keep you poor.

---

1. Not a fair comparison but a fun one: $34 in 1994 could have purchased 30 shares of Apple stock (when it was $1.11 per share). I would have had $0.70 left over, which I could have used to purchase one pack of baseball cards. (It would have had a stick of gum, too, which didn't come with the complete sets.) If I held on to them both, in May 2020, I would have a handful of baseball cards worth about $0.65 and $9,643.50 worth of Apple stock (30 shares at $321.45 per share).

PART I
THE 401(k)

CHAPTER 1

A HISTORY OF TAXATION AND A BRIEF REVIEW OF BASIC ECONOMICS

"The difference between death and taxes is death doesn't get worse every time Congress meets."

—WILL ROGERS

EVERYONE HAS HEARD OF A 401(K). That's not surprising considering that 55 million Americans have about $5.8 trillion in 401(k) plans.[1] That's $5,800,000,000,000.00! Of course, our minds fall well short of being able to conceptualize numbers in the trillions, so let's put that into perspective: if you were to start with $5.8 trillion and spend one million dollars every day, it would take you 15,890 years and 150 days to run out.

Under that scenario, if you had started your lavish spending the same time the Egyptians started building their pyramids, right now you would be 29 percent done and have 11,270 years left. And that's assuming you aren't earning any interest on your money. Because if you're earning any more than 0.000017 percent on your $5.8 trillion,[2] then you could spend a million dollars every day and never run out.[3]

The 401(k) is so ubiquitous that it is probably hard to believe that it did not exist before 1978.[4] But before you start (or continue) sticking your money

---

1. Once the new numbers come out from the COVID-19 related stock market drop, that number is going to be significantly lower due to the withdrawals people are making from their 401(k)s and because the value of their balances has fallen.

2. This makes even the interest rate on your savings account look generous.

3. If you've ever seen *Brewster's Millions*, you'll understand that spending this much money is not as easy (or as fun) as it sounds.

4. Throughout this book, I will be discussing 401(k)s specifically, but the general principles and attributes (and shortfalls and limitations) apply equally to other qualified plans, including IRAs, SEPs, TSPs, 457 Plans, 529s, etc.

into a 401(k) plan, it's worth discovering exactly what you're doing with your money. And that requires us to look into the 401(k)'s backstory.

The history of the 401(k) is necessarily a history of taxes.

A BRIEF HISTORY OF TAXES IN AMERICA

As Americans, aversion to taxes is in our blood. Our nation was born in response to what we perceived as blatant and onerous taxation.[5] Such is our aversion that the federal government has had to get creative when it imposes new taxes, or we would never stand for it.[6] Let's review some tax history[7]:

Although Americans were paying taxes before they even declared their independence from Britain, taxation was far different than it is now. There were several significant actions of the British that ultimately resulted in war and American independence, both of which had to do with taxes.

Great Britain passed the Stamp Act of 1765, which mandated that certain papers in the American colonies (including legal documents, newspapers, pamphlets, and playing cards) have a tax stamp affixed to it. These stamps were purchased from Britain, and the tax revenue went into the king's coffers.

---

5. And which, if given a choice, any one of us would immediately accept in lieu of the current tax code.
6. You may recall President Barack Obama promising that his Affordable Care Act was not a tax (and why would he say anything different? No one wants to raise taxes!). However, the United States Supreme Court, when asked to decide whether Obamacare was constitutional, reached the divided conclusion that it was but only because it was a tax and fell within the federal government's constitutional authority to levy taxes. *Nat'l Fed'n of Indep. Bus. v. Sebelius*, 567 U.S. 519, 132 S. Ct. 2566, 183 L. Ed. 2d 450 (2012). That's no different than the marketing team of a company promising one thing while the fulfillment team clarifies, "Now that you've bought the product, that's not really how it works." In legal terms, we call that fraud.
7. To be fair, this is not just an American thing. Onerous taxation may have been the spark that lit the fire that became the inferno America is now, but tax revolt is as human as anything. There were large-scale tax revolts in the Later Han dynasty in Asia (AD 25–220), in Babylon during Hammurabi's reign (1792–1750 BC), and against the Roman Empire in Europe (27 BC–AD 337). Burg, David F., *A World History of Tax Rebellions* (Routledge, NY 2004), preface.

Britain, for its part, justified the tax on the high cost of British military protection for the colonists at the conclusion of the Seven Years' War. The real reason for the tax was likely the post-war debt that saddled Britain. The colonists strongly opposed British Parliament imposing any taxes without allowing the colonists a voice in parliament. Parliament refused to listen, so the colonists issued a refrain that would echo through history: "No taxation without representation."

The Stamp Act largely failed. In an attempt to raise more revenue and to legitimize through precedent Britain's right to tax the colonies, British Parliament passed the Townsend Acts in 1767 and 1768. These acts, among other things, imposed duties on British products that colonists were only allowed to purchase from Britain, including glass, lead, paints, paper, and tea. To enforce these new acts, Britain created the American Customs Board in Boston.

The Bostonians strongly opposed the presence of the American Customs Board. Their opposition was such that Britain sent in military aid. This escalation eventually resulted in the Boston Massacre.

Just a few years later, Britain passed the Tea Act of 1773, the last in our trilogy of tax acts. It aimed to rescue the failing British East India Tea Company by allowing it to sell its tea directly to the colonies without first going through London (eliminating the middle man) and without having to pay a duty on the tea. The British hoped this act would undercut the Dutch, who were selling tea to the colonists at much lower prices through what the British considered smuggling activity. The colonists perceived this tax, which was still not accompanied by colonial representation in Parliament, as an attempt to legitimize the tea taxes in the Townsend Acts. The colonists famously boarded three tea-laden ships on a winter night in Boston Harbor and dumped the tea into the sea.

These taxes, and the colonists' responses to the taxes, precipitated the Declaration of Independence and the Revolutionary War. For a time, the only taxes the United States levied were on foreigners through tariffs and other customs charges. Think about that. The Founding Fathers were so opposed to taxes that they refused to tax their own citizens.[8]

> ### *The Founding Fathers were so opposed to taxes that they refused to tax their own citizens.*

Due to the Revolutionary War, though, the fledgling United States was in debt. A few years after the country was formed, Alexander Hamilton proposed the first taxation on an American product that Americans would have to pay: an excise tax of seven cents for every gallon of whiskey sold. His proposal became law in 1791. Again, Americans swiftly reacted in the protracted Whiskey Rebellion, a resistance to the tax that lasted three years and often became violent.

Since that first excise tax, the government has come up with new and creative ways to collect revenue. Americans have become more tolerant of taxes in all their forms, and our reactions have become less swift and less severe.[9]

The Income Tax Chronology

Believe it or not, income tax did not exist in any form prior to 1861. However, to generate revenue to fund the Civil War (and to make up for lost tariffs for products shipped to the South), Congress passed the Revenue Act of 1861, which imposed a 3 percent tax on all income over $800. This act and its progeny were repealed in 1872.

The 1894 Tariff Act once again imposed an income tax. But just a year later, the United States Supreme Court issued a decision, *Pollock v. Farmers'*

---

8. Of course, such magnanimity wouldn't last.
9. Cliven Bundy is one notable exception. Bundy was a Nevada cattle rancher who did not believe that the federal government had the authority to charge him grazing fees when his cattle grazed on federal land. He became a symbol for proponents of small government and a catalyst in a standoff between the federal government (Bureau of Land Management law enforcement and FBI agents) and hundreds of militiamen in what has since become known as the Battle of Bunkerville.

Loan & Trust Co. This decision recognized constitutional limitations (having to do with apportionment, which was a requirement that each state's population be taken into account) on how the government could enforce that tax law. *Pollock* made collection impractical and effectively nullified the income taxes associated with the 1894 Tariff Act.

In an effort to open the door to broader taxation, Congress proposed an amendment to the Constitution that would allow income taxation without apportionment. That proposal was ratified as the Sixteenth Amendment in 1913,[10] which was followed immediately by the Revenue Act of 1913.

The Revenue Act imposed a 1 percent tax on income above $3,000 and 6 percent tax on income above $500,000. That doesn't sound too bad, does it? Those amounts were increased in 1918 to fund the First World War, at which point all income over one million dollars was taxed at a rate of 77 percent! That went down to 58 percent in 1922, 25 percent in 1925, and 24 percent in 1929.

The Great Depression saw the need for high taxation again when an astounding 94 percent of income above $200,000 went back to the government in taxes. Although the Constitution protects against cruel and unusual punishment, few are the safeguards against onerous and excessive taxation.

To help fund World War II, quarterly tax collection was introduced, as was payroll withholding. These did not represent tax increases but put the taxes in the government's coffers sooner. As a result, money could no longer be used by individuals and businesses after the revenue was collected and before the taxes had to be paid.

Between the end of the Second Great War and the end of the 1970s, the federal income tax rate for the highest-grossing earners in the nation was never lower than 70 percent.

---

10. "The Congress shall have power to lay and collect taxes on incomes, from whatever source derived, without apportionment among the several States, and without regard to any census or enumeration."

Enter the 1980s. The Economic Recovery Tax Act of 1981 lowered the highest tax rate down to about 50 percent, and the Tax Reform Act of 1986 lowered it again to 28 percent.

The government in the 1980s was able to successfully market their changes as a reduction in taxes. However, we can't forget the most basics in a balanced budget, which applies in a single home or a national fund: there are only two sides of a ledger—money coming in and money going out. To keep a budget balanced, you must have more money coming in than going out.

A BRIEF REVIEW
OF BASIC ECONOMICS

There are basically two ways to make sure you have positive cash flow: (1) increase the amount of money coming in or (2) decrease the amount of money going out.

You don't have to be Robert Kiyosaki or Warren Buffett to figure this out. Millions of families already understand this. Let's say a family's expenses go up, like when they have a new child (or taxes increase or inflation decreases the value of their dollar or there are unforeseen medical bills or house repairs, etc.) For a family living hand to mouth, this means they either need to come up with a way to make more money, or they need to cut expenses elsewhere.

If you haven't had personal experience with a tight budget, you have at least seen it portrayed on screen. This is a common trope in television and movies: one member of a two-income household wants to quit the job they hate to pursue a dream of becoming a [insert high-risk, high-reward dream job here, like sports star, author, musician, or other kind of artist]. The other, wanting to be supportive, agrees to pick up a few extra shifts at work to make up the difference. Because that's not going to be enough, they also let the housekeeper go, trade in the fancy car for something more practical, and start eating dinner at home instead of out. (The reason this scenario is common in television is that it is common in real life—and it creates tension, and therefore, drama.)

All they're doing is trying to increase the money coming in, decrease the money going out, or both.

And although we don't typically think about the federal government the same way we think about balancing our own household budget, it is similar but with a few very important distinctions.

The first thing you have to understand is that unlike your household, the government is not part of a producing market. Whatever job you have, you are providing some sort of product or service (or both), and you are paid for adding value to individuals, businesses, and the economy. This is true for your teenage son who started his own car-detailing business; for your spouse, who waits tables part time while going to school; and for you, who sells houses. Consider for a moment:

Your teenager spends his days washing, waxing, polishing, drying, vacuuming, and otherwise detailing vehicles.[11] What he does is part of an open and competitive market that relies on differences in valuation between the purchaser and the seller.

Let's say your son charges one hundred dollars to detail the typical sedan. To the sedan-owner client, having a clean, fresh-smelling car is worth more than the hundred dollars she has to give up to have your son detail her car.

To your son, though, the one hundred dollars is worth more to him than the time and effort it takes to detail a sedan. Based on differing values, both sides are getting more than they receive from the same transaction. The transaction moves forward, and the economy gets a tiny boost.

That's how the market works. If your son couldn't find enough people who value a clean car more than one hundred dollars, then he'd have to lower his

---

11. A more likely scenario is that your teenager spends his days playing video games, but if you aren't one of those parents who has a go-getting, entrepreneurial teenage son, let's pretend for a moment that you do.

prices. But if the price had to be lower than what it was worth for him to detail a car, then he would most likely choose to stop detailing cars. He would sell his business, hire an employee to do it for cheaper (and therefore make it worth it again), find some other way to increase the value of what he offers (or decrease the cost), or go spend his time doing something else.

This is where competition becomes very important. If your son is the only person in town detailing cars, then he's going to be able to charge more than he would otherwise. Maybe he can charge $150, or even $200. That's good for your son but bad for everyone else who is either paying more than they would otherwise for the service or not getting the service at all. Maybe it's more than they want to or can afford to pay. Or maybe because your son is the only guy in town doing it, the demand far exceeds the supply, since he can't service everyone in town who wants their car detailed. Because he has no competition, maybe he doesn't try as hard to do a good job as he would if customers were more difficult to come by.

This lack of competition creates opportunity for others. A local neighborhood girl notices the lack of supply and opens her own car detailing business. If your son is charging $150, then she's going to start charging $125.

If quality is comparable to your son's (or even if it is slightly worse), some people are going to start using her services instead of your son's. This requires your son to make some changes to generate the same amount of profit. He'll either have to offer more for the same price or lower his prices. Maybe he'll start offering a rainy-day guarantee where he promises a free exterior wash if it rains within a week of the detailing job. Or maybe he'll just lower his price to be more competitive. The more people there are offering these services, the more your son is going to have to worry about quality and price.

Competition may frustrate your son, and it may cause him to work harder than he would otherwise, but it's good for the community. It provides consumers with choices and different price points. Furthermore, it incentivizes him—and the other car detailers—to make quality a priority.

Unfortunately, these truths of the open market just don't apply to the federal government. The government is not trying to provide the best service so you'll spend your money with them instead of with someone else. It is not trying to win you over with its amazing customer service or short wait times. It is not competing at all. It is not engaging in value exchanges. Governments do not earn money. They take money.

The federal government only has those powers that the U.S. Constitution specifically grants to it, which means its power is limited.[12] (The states, on the other hand, have plenary power, which means they have power over things not specifically listed in the country's founding document.) One of those powers is the source of the federal government's income: the power to "lay and collect taxes, duties, imposts, and exises [sic]."[13]

If you get anything out of this chapter, this is the part you'll want to remember: Government does not "earn" its own money or income. It takes its money from its citizens through taxation.

Government does not "earn" its own money or income. It takes its money from its citizens through taxation.

So where does the 401(k) come into play in all of this? In 1978, the promise of a large tax reduction materialized in the form of a congressional bill. There were several provisions related to tax brackets, personal exemptions, and tax deductions that received the most attention with this proposed law. But hidden among those other changes were a few paragraphs that would arguably become the most sweeping and far-reaching revision in decades, which at the time, no one really noticed: Congress amended section 401 of the tax code—the section addressing taxation of qualified pension, profit-sharing, and stock bonus plans.

---

12. Those specific enumerated powers have been interpreted more and more broadly over the years, giving the federal government more power even without amending the Constitution, but that's a discussion for another time.
13. U.S. Const. Art I § 8.

They stuck 864 words between existing subsections (k) and (l) and created a new subsection (k): 26 U.S.C. 401(k).[14]

This new set of laws would change the landscape of taxation, and if not taxation, then at least the landscape of retirement. It allowed employees under certain circumstances to defer taxation on income until retirement.

This was a novel yet largely ignored idea at the time. Pre-1980, employees were not accustomed to funding their own retirement.[15] Their pensions were mostly employer funded. But in 1980, a financial consultant named Ted Benna realized the potential of the new language in 26 U.S.C. 401(k). Although his approach was not expressly contemplated by the new law, Benna worked with his clients to set up plans where employers would match benefits to encourage their employees to use their own money to contribute to retirement plans and be able to use pretax dollars to do it.

Participating employees would immediately see two benefits to contributing: they would (1) get a tax deduction for every dollar contributed and (2) see immediate returns in the form of employer contributions. As the 401(k) became better known, employees started to contribute.

Under the new 401(k) plan, the employers were the real winners, though. Under the pension plans, which were typically defined-benefit plans, the employers would guarantee a definite postretirement income for their employees, which was based on the employee's salary and how long the employee had been working for the company. Employees could look up their pensions at any time and see exactly how much of a retirement salary they had earned.

Of course, these defined-benefit pension plans were great for the employees but not so great for the employers. The employers had to manage their money in such a way that there would be enough to fund the employee's retirement; all the investment risk fell on the employer.

14. *See* 26 U.S.C. 401(k) legislative history, particularly the Revenue Act of 1978.
15. Arguably, most people now aren't either. But they no longer have employer-funded pensions to rely on.

The employers knew how much they had to contribute postretirement on a monthly basis. They had no idea, though, what the total contribution would be over the employee's lifetime because of one huge unknowable factor—how long the employee would live past retirement. The employer could be facing a relatively small debt or, if the employee lived a long time, a huge monetary commitment.

What few realized at the time was just how much of a burden these pensions would create in the long run. When asked the cause of its closure in 2018, Sears's CEO blamed the $300 million that Sears was paying per year toward its former employees' pensions.[16] The U.S. Post Office is facing a similar future considering its $120 billion in unfunded post-employment liabilities.[17]

These new 401(k) plans were not defined-*benefit* plans, but were defined-*contribution* plans, meaning that the monthly retirement benefit was not known or defined. Only the amount going into the plan—the contribution—was known and defined.

This was a big win for employers, and their stockholders loved it. Instead of promising an unknown, possibly huge number to employees and then managing money well enough to be able to meet those obligations, now the employers paid a little money now and their obligation was met.

This shift transferred two burdens to the employee: the burden of payment and the burden of risk. The employees were the losers here, and not just because they were now paying the bill the employer used to pay and taking the risk the employer used to take. Employees were the big losers here because 401(k)s are a bad deal.[18]

And that, if you'll allow the pedestrian eloquence, is the thesis of Part I: 401(k)s are a bad deal.

---

16. Chris Isidore, "What's Killing Sears? Its Own Retirees, the CEO Says," CNN Business, September 14, 2018, last accessed July 8, 2020, https://money.cnn.com/2018/09/14/news/companies/sears-pension-retirees/index.html.

17. "U.S. Postal Service Reports Fiscal Year 2019 Results," USPS, November 14, 2019, last accessed July 8, 2020, https://about.usps.com/newsroom/national-releases/2019/1114-usps-reports-fiscal-year-2019-results.htm.

18. I hope this little spoiler doesn't ruin the end of the book for you. Let's just call it heavy foreshadowing.

CHAPTER 2

IF THE 401(K) WERE A CIVIL CONTRACT, IT WOULD BE UNENFORCEABLE

"The greater danger for most of us lies not in setting our aim too high and falling short; but in setting our aim too low and achieving our mark."

—MICHELANGELO

NOW THAT WE'VE REVIEWED the history of taxation in this country, gone over the basics of economics, and witnessed the birth of the 401(k), we're ready to dive in. Let's start with a brief summary of what you already know.

A 401(k) is a voluntary agreement you make with Uncle Sam. And like any other agreement, both sides are promising something in exchange for the other side's promise. For your part, you agree to all of the following:

- You will not put in more than a certain amount each year.[1]

- Once the money is in the account, you will only invest in certain things (i.e., you will not put the money in what the IRS calls "prohibited transactions").[2]

- The money you invest will most likely be in stocks and bonds, and therefore subject to market volatility.[3]

---

1. This amount is always changing, but as of 2020, for a 401(k), 403(b), and most 457 plans, it is $19,500 for single people, with another $6,500 for those at least 50 years old. The limit for IRAs is $6,000 with an extra $1,000 allowed for people 50 years old and older.
2. IRS Publication 590-A (2019), IRS.gov, last accessed July 8, 2020, https://www.irs.gov/publications/p590a (once at this page, click on the link for "Prohibited Transactions" in the table of contents).
3. For the more-savvy investor, there are ways to set up 401(k) accounts so you can invest in other things, like real estate.

- You will not withdraw any of your money until you are 59½ years old, or if you do, you will pay a 10 percent penalty *and* taxes on the money you withdraw.[4]

- When you turn seventy-two, you must start withdrawing a minimum amount annually as determined by the government whether you want to or not (called "required minimum distributions" or "RMDs"), which is a rate you cannot negotiate.

- When you take your withdrawal, whether limited to the RMDs or some greater amount, you will pay taxes on 100 percent of the money. This includes the money you originally put in and all the growth you've seen since at a rate determined by the government, which rate you cannot negotiate.

- If you are an employer and want to set up a plan, you cannot make it available just for you because you cannot discriminate. You have to contribute for others you employ, too, and in proportionate amounts.

In exchange for that agreement, Uncle Sam agrees not to tax you on any money you put into the plan this year, thereby reducing your taxable income. They'll catch the taxes on the backend at whatever rate they set in the future.

When you spell it out like that, it doesn't seem like a very fair agreement, does it? Indeed, if a 401(k) were a civil contract, I daresay it would not be enforceable.

An enforceable legal contract has three elements—an offer, an acceptance, and consideration.[5] Put in nonlegal terms, that means one party has to promise something, the other party accepts the promise, and both promises are made for

---

4. The government made a temporary exception to the early withdrawal penalties in the midst of the Covid-19 craziness, but the withdrawer has to pay taxes on the withdrawal within three years. Plus, that "gift," like all others from the government, comes at a cost.
5. Different states have different laws regarding contracts, but as to these elements, there is little variation. *See, e.g., Baker v. Bristol Care, Inc.,* 450 S.W.3d 770, 774 (Mo. 2014).

the purpose of inducing the other promise. This mutual inducement has a legal name: consideration.

Although the definition is simple, in application, it becomes quite a bit more complicated. The concept of consideration, or a "bargained-for-exchange," is one that frustrates many a law student.

We aren't going to get into it much here, except to explore one manifestation of a failure of consideration, which makes a promise void and unenforceable. It is something called an "illusory promise."[6]

401(K) AS AN ILLUSORY PROMISE

For a contract to be enforceable, there must be a mutuality of promises that are both definite enough that they are capable of being enforced and contain enough commitment that a promise is actually being made.

As one legal treatise puts it, "One of the commonest kind[s] of promises too indefinite for legal enforcement is where the promisor retains an unlimited right to decide later the nature or extent of his performance. This unlimited choice in effect destroys the promise and makes it merely illusory."[7]

GEICO—yes, that car insurance company represented by a little green gecko and which, appropriate to our discussion, stands for Government Employees Insurance Company—will serve as our example due to their use of illusory promises in an insurance policy that was scrutinized in at least one published case.

In 2017, an Illinois appellate court had to decide whether GEICO's contractual promises included consideration or whether they were merely illusory and therefore, unenforceable.

GEICO's insured, a Florida resident named Evan Fronauer, was in a car crash in Illinois with two women who claimed injury. Fronauer submitted the

---

6. 2 J. Perillo & H. Bender, Corbin on Contracts, § 5.28, at 142 (1995).
7. 1 Williston, Contracts s 43 (3rd ed.).

claim to GEICO, his insurer, and GEICO denied the claim based on the out-of-state coverage provision exception in the policy.

In this provision, GEICO promised to provide out-of-state coverage to the extent required by Illinois law (which requires mandatory bodily injury liability coverage). But then after that promise, at the end, the policy says, "We will not provide coverage for injury to a person, caused by accident, including resulting sickness, disease or death."

So out of one side of its mouth, GEICO promised coverage, but out of the other, it promised not to provide coverage.

The Illinois court looked at this and saw it for what it was: an illusory promise. "The fourth sentence of GEICO's out-of-state coverage endorsement revealed, contrary to the first sentence's promise, that GEICO has not committed itself to providing bodily injury liability coverage to the extent required by Illinois law. The result is that the promise of coverage contained in the out-of-state coverage endorsement was illusory and void in this case."[8]

When I teach this concept in my paralegal courses, I show the students a clip from *Shrek 2* where Shrek, having been magically converted from an ogre to a dashing human, is looking for clothes for his new body. He, Puss in Boots, and Donkey (who had become a magnificent steed) hold up a carriage and steal a man's clothing. After the exchange and just before riding off into the horizon, Shrek makes what amounts to an illusory promise: "Thank you, gentlemen. Someday I will repay you, unless, of course, I can't find you or if I forget."[9] That's what GEICO did leading up to the 2017 Illinois case, and that's what the government does with your 401(k) retirement money.

In effect, "[a]n illusory promise is an expression cloaked in promissory terms, but which, upon closer examination, reveals that the promisor has committed himself not at all."[10]

---

8. *Am. Access Cas. Co. v. Mendoza*, 2017 IL App (1st) 170354-U, ¶ 23.
9. *Shrek 2*, ©2004.
10. J. Calamari & J. Perillo, Contracts, § 70, at 133 (1970).

If we scrutinize your agreement with Uncle Sam, there are at least two illusory promises that would be voided if this were a contract: taxation upon withdrawal and RMDs.

Illusory Promise in Taxation upon Withdrawals

Remember, the government promises not to tax the money now in exchange for taxing you later. But they don't tell you what the taxes will be later. Put another way, with a 401(k), what Uncle Sam is really promising you is this: "When you withdraw your money in the future, we will charge you whatever the tax rate is at the time. We have sole authority to choose what that tax rate is—you don't get to negotiate it—and you will pay it."

> **With a 401(k), what Uncle Sam is really promising you is this: "When you withdraw your money in the future, we will charge you whatever the tax rate is at the time. We have sole authority to choose what that tax rate is—you don't get to negotiate it—and you will pay it."**

Let's compare that to the definition of an illusory promise: "where the promisor retains an unlimited right to decide later the nature or extent of his performance."[11]

The U.S. government is retaining "an unlimited right to decide later the nature or extent of [its] performance." It gets to choose what you pay later on.

Imagine if that were part of any other arrangement. You go into a car dealership to lease a car. You promise to make monthly payments for three years, and they promise that the monthly payments will be "$300 or whatever they decide to change it to at a later date."

---

11. 1 Williston, Contracts s 43 (3rd ed.).

You finance the purchase of a house. The bank promises to finance it at whatever interest rate they choose, which rate you will discover after you sign the contract.

Would you ever enter into an agreement like that? No way!

But that's exactly what the government is promising us. I heard one person put it this way:

> A 401(k) is basically the government coming to you and offering to go into business with you. They say, "You put up all the money; you take all the risk, and in thirty years, I'll tell you how much you owe me."[12]

Isn't that exactly what the government is offering you?

Illusory Promise with RMDs

The second illusory promise the government makes has to do with the RMDs. Remember, when you turn a certain age (for now that age is seventy-two), you have to start taking out a certain minimum and then pay taxes on it. But the government leaves those terms open ended too. They don't tell you how much that will be, or at what age, until you get there.

In fact, with the passage of the SECURE Act, which became effective at the end of 2019, the age changed from 70½ to 72 years old. Most people viewed that as a good thing because it gave the 401(k) owner an extra year and a half to choose what to do with their money. But Congress doesn't just give anything away for free. There were strings attached.

What most people are not aware of is that the government, to make up for the revenue they would lose from people not taking their RMDs during that year and a half, changed the rules for people who would inherit these qualified plans.

---

12. I heard this at a seminar put on by Larry McClean of Your Family Bank in St. Augustine, Florida, in the first quarter of 2018.

Under the old rule, any money left in your 401(k) when you die would pass to your heirs.[13] They would then make withdrawals as they desired, and whatever they withdrew would be added to their taxable income.[14] Now, they must withdraw the entire amount within ten years.

That change is significant. Before, the heirs had broader flexibility when strategizing the best way to make withdrawals so it had a minimum effect on their taxable income. Now they must accelerate their plans and withdraw it within ten years—which may be in high-income years when their tax burden is going to be the heaviest.

The government makes no promises when it comes to what the RMDs will be for you. It doesn't promise the age when they'll be required. It doesn't promise how much will be required to be withdrawn. That's another illusory promise—the government gets to decide when you have to start withdrawing *your* money and how much you have to withdraw. The more we learn, the less it feels like it's yours, right?

401(k) as an Illusory Promise as a Whole

Although I've highlighted two elements of a 401(k) known to change—tax rates and RMD provisions—the truth is, the government is not really making any promises beyond the fact that you can defer tax payment for contributions to your qualified plan. It could change the tax code at any time and in any way. All that money you've put away for retirement is going to be subject to whatever changes it decides to make.

This is not just hypothetical. The changes to the tax code in the SECURE Act discussed above are just one example of recent changes. But of all the

---

13. It would have converted to an IRA when you stopped working.
14. The rules weren't quite that simple—there was still a minimum amount that had to be withdrawn, after a maximum of five years being left untouched, but the heirs had a lot of flexibility. The rule was a little different if it was a spouse inheriting the IRA—they could just roll it into their own and follow the same rules that applied to theirs.

United States statutes, the tax code is perhaps the most fluid. By one estimate, in the ten years between 2009 and 2019, the tax code was amended or revised over 4,000 times![15]

By one estimate, in the ten years between 2009 and 2019, the tax code was amended or revised over 4,000 times!

That's almost incomprehensible. On average, that's more than one revision every day for ten years straight. No wonder it's so hard to understand. It's a moving target.

That 10 percent penalty for early withdrawals? Could become anything.

The 59½ age limit for withdrawals? Could be changed to anything.

The limits on what you can invest in? Yep, that can change, too.

We don't know what the future holds. We don't know what crazy ideas our representatives might get in their heads. But we do know that the U.S. Government consistently spends more than it collects. (That's the growing trillion-dollar deficit you keep hearing about).

So what do you think is more likely—the government starts to spend less to operate within its means, or the government increases its "earnings" by raising taxes? How confident are you that they won't try to tap into the excess of $5,000,000,000,000 (that's $5 trillion) that people currently have in their 401(k) plans?

Put yourself in the government's shoes. You and your spouse are discussing the budget. You have two options: you can earn more money, or you can spend less. You talk about trading in your nice car for something more practical. You talk about cancelling Netflix. Yes, they're doable, but you don't really want to. Then you realize that to make more money, you don't have to work harder,

---

15. eFile, "US Income Tax History, Taxucation," October 29, 2019, last accessed July 8, 2020, https://www.efile.com/tax-history-and-the-tax-code/.

you just have to give yourself a raise. Your employer may not be happy, but he'll have to pay.

Yeah, that sounds ridiculous, but that's exactly the discussion Congress has every time they look at the budget. They could cut back on government programs and agencies. They could try to be more efficient. Or they could just give themselves a raise (i.e., raise taxes). Their boss (you and other taxpayers) may not like it, but we'll have to pay it.

That doesn't sound fair, but that's reality. You certainly can't fall back on contractual principles because, illusory promise or not, once you put your money in a 401(k), the government gets to choose what happens with your money.

> *Once you put your money in a 401(k), the government gets to choose what happens with your money.*

401(K) AS AN UNCONSCIONABLE CONTRACT

Another important doctrine in the law of contracts is unconscionability. Unconscionability is a principle that allows a court to invalidate an otherwise enforceable agreement because the agreement, in good consciousness, should not be enforced.

Unconscionability is a two-pronged analysis. The courts will consider whether the contract or provision is procedurally unconscionable and whether it is substantively unconscionable. It must be both procedurally and substantively unconscionable for the provision to be invalidated.[16]

---

16. This is another contractual principal that will vary state to state but which is largely universal. *See, e.g., Strand v. U.S. Bank Nat. Ass'n ND*, 2005 ND 68, ¶ 4, 693 N.W.2d 918, 921.

Procedural Unconscionability

Procedural unconscionability measures abuses arising out of the formation of the contract.[17] Some of the trappings of procedural unconscionability include contract language that is hard to understand, important provisions written in small print,[18] unequal bargaining power between the parties, or misleading language that disguises the consequences of the contract.[19]

One hallmark of unequal bargaining power comes in the form of an adhesion contract—a nonnegotiable, take-it-or-leave it contract that "leaves the weaker party no choice as to its terms."[20]

If we were to organize these requirements, we could put them into two categories with several things to look for in each category:

1. Was the non-drafting party given a meaningful opportunity to understand the contract?
   a. Is the contract easy to understand?
   b. Is there misleading language?
   c. Are there important provisions hidden in the text or in small print?
   d. Are there terms in use that only the drafter of the contract, being more sophisticated, would understand, like terms of the trade or technical terms?
   e. Was the non-drafting party given an opportunity to read the contract?
2. Was the non-drafting party given a meaningful opportunity to negotiate the contract?

---

17. *E.g., Strand* 693 N.W.2d 918 at 921.
18. *E.g., Glassford v. BrickKicker*, 2011 VT 118, ⁋ 27, 191 Vt. 1, 15, 35 A.3d 1044, 1053 (2011).
19. *E.g., D.R. Horton, Inc. v. Green*, 120 Nev. 549, 554, 96 P.3d 1159, 1162 (2004), overruled on other grounds by *U.S. Home Corp. v. Michael Ballesteros Tr.*, 134 Nev. 180, 415 P.3d 32 (2018).
20. *Burch v. Second Judicial Dist. Court of State ex rel. Cty. of Washoe*, 118 Nev. 438, 442, 49 P.3d 647, 649 (2002).

ZACHARIAH B. PARRY

a. Was the contract one of adhesion, given without any power to negotiate?

b. Was one party in a weaker bargaining position, either because of a power imbalance or difference in sophistication?

If the 401(k) were a contract, its language would be that found in 26 U.S.C. 401(k).

Let's use it as an example and do a legal analysis of procedural unconscionability.

Meaningful Opportunity to Understand the Contract

First was the non-drafting party (you, the 401[k] investor) given a meaningful opportunity to understand the contract?

Well, let's evaluate part of the statute to see if its meaning is clear. Remember how when the 401(k) was introduced in 1978, it had 864 words? Since then, with all the changes it has undergone, it is now a 5,321-word behemoth. [21] Length alone will not invalidate a contract, but just for fun, go look up the statute and start reading it.[22] See how far you get before you realize two things: (1) you really don't understand it at all, and (2) what you do understand bears no resemblance to what you know about 401(k)s.

Before we look at the actual language, let's run it through some readability algorithms. The Flesch Reading Ease algorithm analyzes written passages to determine how easy the text can be understood. The scores range from 0.0 to 100.00.[23] The higher the number, the more readable the text. A score of 90–100 means the text is probably easily understood by a fifth grader. A score of 30–50 means it is

---

21. To be fair, the extra words don't necessarily make it any harder to read than the 1978 version. If you look up the original version, you'll see it wasn't any clearer.
22. Yeah, "fun" doesn't mean what I think it means, I know.
23. The way the algorithm works, you could actually get scores below 0 or above 100, but those would be extremely rare.

difficult to read and probably requires a partial college education. Anything below 30 is very difficult to read and probably only understandable to university graduates. The Flesch-Kincaid Grade Level algorithm is similar but assigns a grade-level score that represents the lowest grade level that is likely to understand the text.

The first paragraph in the Introduction of this book has a Flesch Reading Ease score of 69.81 (probably easily understood by an eighth grader) and a Flesch-Kincaid Grade Level score of 9.9 (probably understood by someone finishing their ninth-grade year).

The sentence "It was the best of times, it was the worst of times ..." scores 100 on the Flesch Reading Ease test (a fifth grader could understand it) and 0.89 on the Flesch-Kincaid Grade Level test (a kindergartner/first grader could understand it).[24] The Pledge of Allegiance scores 38.92 (college level) and 15.53 (college level), respectively.

To protect against insurers abusing their insureds, many states are now requiring that insurance policies meet a minimum readability score on the Flesch-Kincaid readability test. For example, Florida and New York require insurance policies to have a minimum score of 45.[25] Maine requires a readability score of 50.[26] The first paragraph of this book and the first line of a *Tale of Two Cities* would pass those tests. The Pledge of Allegiance is too low (and if you review it in your head and try and parse out exactly what it means, particularly the last part, you'll understand why).

So, let's look at the first paragraph (which is all one sentence) of 26 U.S.C. 401(k)(1). This was likely as far as you got if you actually did the exercise and started reading the statute:

A profit-sharing or stock bonus plan, a pre-ERISA money purchase plan, or a rural cooperative plan shall not be considered as

---

24. The first line in Charles Dickens's *Tale of Two Cities*.
25. Fla. Stat. § 627.4145; NY Insurance § 3102(c)(D).
26. Me. Stat. tit. 24-A § 2441(1)(A).

not satisfying the requirements of subsection (a) merely because the plan includes a qualified cash or deferred arrangement.

This produces a Flesch Reading Ease score of 16.65! If the algorithm is right, this paragraph requires a university graduate to understand.[27] The Flesch-Kincaid Grade Level score is 21.12, which represents someone nine years into college.[28]

These algorithms alone tell us that this first paragraph/sentence is not easily understood. Don't forget, several states require insurance policies to have a minimum readability score of 45–50.[29] This is not even close. If they're going to write a statute that requires an advanced degree to understand, then it seems only fair that it should not apply to anyone who doesn't have an advanced degree.[30] But let's actually look at its content ourselves to see if it is easy or hard to understand.

The subject of the sentence references three types of plans that appear to have nothing to do with the money you, as an employee, put away every year toward your retirement: (1) profit-sharing or stock bonus plan, (2) pre-ERISA money purchase plan, and (3) rural cooperative plan. So what are those, and what do they have to do with your 401(k) retirement plan?

Let's start with "profit-sharing or stock bonus plan." A thorough search through the rest of the statute reveals that although this term is used frequently enough, it is never defined. Alas, maybe we'll have better luck with the other two.

---

27. I have both an undergraduate degree and a postgraduate degree and am an author and an editor who owns and operates a tax law firm. I've spent a long time reading this sentence, and I'm not confident I fully understand what it means.

28. Someone nine years into college better be a medical student, or they're probably not the ones contemplated by this readability algorithm.

29. For all of these tests, I used the Readability Analyzer published by Datayze.com at https://datayze.com/readability-analyzer, last accessed April 21, 2020.

30. Ha! If only logic and fairness entered the equation. Actually, I have an advanced degree. So maybe not.

"Pre-ERISA money purchase plan" is defined in 26 U.S.C. 401(k)(6), which relies on 26 U.S.C. 414(i) to define it. ERISA itself is the Employee Retirement Income Security Act, which is another federal statute, 29 U.S.C. 18. So before we even get started, we apparently have to have some understanding of that feature-length statute.

Both "rural cooperative" and "rural cooperative plan" are defined in 26 U.S.C. 401(k)(7), which refers to 26 U.S.C. 414(i) for its definition.

Let's look at the next part:

... shall not be considered as not satisfying ...

Hmm. That's a double negative. So does that mean "should be considered as satisfying"? If so, wouldn't it be better to say "satisfies"? Or is it just saying that the inclusion of a qualified cash or deferred arrangement (the last line of the paragraph) alone does not disqualify one of these plans from section (a)? Probably the second. So let's just say that.

Moving on:

... the requirements of subsection (a) ...

Thus begins our third reliance to other statutory language in the first sentence. This refers to subsection (a) of the same section we're in, so 401(a).

Okay. Let's scroll up the nearly 2,000 words to section (a), which itself is a 9,721-word monster.[31] Let's skip it for now because that's a lot to get through to understand a single sentence.

---

31. For those of you interested in how I know how many words are in these sections, I am just going to the language of the statute, copying the referenced provisions into Microsoft Word. At the bottom of the Word window, on the left, is a word count of the entire document. For comparison's sake, up to this point in this book, starting from the introduction and not counting the footnotes, there are 8,244 words.

... merely because the plan includes a qualified cash or deferred arrangement.

Here, we are in luck because this seems to be simple enough, and for once, the definition is close by. In fact, the very next line in the statute is called "Qualified cash or deferred arrangement" and includes this language:

> A qualified cash or deferred arrangement is any arrangement which is part of a profit-sharing or stock bonus plan, a pre-ERISA money purchase plan, or a rural cooperative plan which meets the requirements of subsection (a).[32]

Uh-oh. Looks like we are in circular-logic territory here. Not sure why we are defining part of (a) by referring to (a).

Let's see if we can distill the original paragraph to its meaning in simple terms:

> The fact that a plan may include a qualified cash or deferred arrangement does not alone disqualify:
> 1. a profit-sharing or stock bonus plan (whatever that means),
> 2. a pre-ERISA money purchase plan (as defined in 26 U.S.C. 401(k)(6), 26 U.S.C. 414(i), and 29 U.S.C. 18), or
> 3. a rural cooperative plan from 26 U.S.C. 401(a).
> A qualified cash or deferred arrangement is any arrangement that is part of (1)–(3) above and meets the requirements of 26 U.S.C. 401(a).

If we were to break it down even more, it looks like the first paragraph of 401(k) says that the three plans mentioned aren't taken out of 401(a) just because they have a qualified cash or deferred arrangement. The second paragraph says

---

32. 26 U.S.C. 401(k)(2).

that a qualified cash or deferred arrangement is anything that meets the requirements of 401(a) and is one of those three plans.

Does your brain hurt yet? Notice we didn't have to scour the statute for a section that was hard to understand. We just started at the beginning. It includes definitional references to five different statutes in three different places, a confusing double negative, and circular definitions. After distilling it, it still doesn't make any sense.

Do you have to read any farther to conclude that the people purchasing these plans are not given a meaningful opportunity to understand what it is they are agreeing to? We are already now in strong procedural unconscionability territory. We don't really have to get into whether there are important provisions hidden, fine print, etc. Assuming the entire statute is just as unintelligible—requiring not just an advanced degree but a statute-specific Rosetta stone—those two requirements are easily met.

What about the second half of the procedural unconscionability analysis where we analyze whether the non-drafting party has a meaningful opportunity to negotiate the contract?

Meaningful Opportunity to Negotiate the Contract

If this were a contract, it would for sure be an adhesion contract—a take-it-or-leave-it scenario where the investor can either contribute to a 401(k) under the terms written or choose to invest elsewhere. The investor cannot negotiate the minimum contributions, the RMD age, the tax rate upon withdrawal, the minimum age for penalty-free withdrawal, etc. The investor cannot negotiate anything at all.

Moreover, there is a disparity in sophistication of the parties. The U.S. Government uses a team of legally trained statute drafters who write using undefined terms, legal language, and internal and external references to statutes that the average consumer can't hope to decipher.

The U.S. Government uses a team of legally trained statute drafters who write using undefined terms, legal language, and internal and external references to statutes that the average consumer can't hope to decipher.

On the whole, then, in this lawyer's opinion, if 26 U.S.C. 401(k) were a contract, it would be procedurally unconscionable.

Substantive Unconscionability

Substantive unconscionability measures substantive abuses related to the terms of the contract.[33] It measures whether a term is overly harsh or one sided.[34]

We don't have to do much of an analysis here. Most of what we would need to discuss has already been said. Refer back to pages 15–16 where we compare everything the 401(k) investor promises with what the government promises. Recall the discussion of an illusory promise.

The investor (which was you) put your money away in hopes of providing for your own retirement. This is not a light endeavor. Retirement income is **money you need to survive** when you are no longer working. In exchange for a tax break now on a small portion of your income, your money is locked away where you can't access it. The government gets to choose what happens to it—how long it's locked away, in what it can be invested in the meantime, how steep the penalty is for early access, and how much you'll have to pay when you pull it out. The investor bears all the risk and has none of the control. The U.S. Government bears none of the risk and has all of the control.

---

33. *E.g., Strand* 693 N.W.2d 918 at 921.
34. *E.g., Serafin v. Balco Properties Ltd., LLC,* 235 Cal. App. 4th 165, 177, 185 Cal. Rptr. 3d 151, 160 (2015).

That would be like if you went to a retail store to buy a bike for your kid, and the store clerk told you that one of the conditions of purchasing the bike would be that you had to give it back when the store asked for it back.

"What do you mean I'd have to give it back?" you ask.

"Well, when we ask for you to return it, you'd have to bring it in," the store clerk responds.

"That makes no sense. That sounds more like a lease."

"We call it a purchase, sir."

"But doesn't that sound more like a lease to you, except that I have no control over the term of the lease?"

"We call it a purchase, sir," the clerk repeats.

"Okay. So if I did *purchase* it, how long would I get to keep the bike?"

"We don't know. Usually people get to keep their bikes for a long time, but it really depends on when we want it back."

"And if you do ask for it back, are you going to give me my money back?" you ask.

"Oh no. All purchases are final."

"Do you come pick it up?"

"No, sir. You would have to drop it off."

"And what if I lose the bike or it gets damaged in the meantime?"

"Then you would have to pay us its value so we can get a new bike," the clerk answers.

"But I would have already paid you."

"Yes, sir. But you would have to pay us again if we ask for it back and you don't return it to us in good quality."

"What if I refuse to give it back?"

"Then we would levy a judgment and put a lien on your house and garnish your wages."

"So why in the world would I buy a bike from you?"

Imagine a similar discussion with the government:

"Wait, you're saying you want me to put my money away in your plan, but then I can't access the money?" you ask.

"No, ma'am. You can access it. You would just have to pay a 10 percent penalty if you access it before you're 59½ years old, unless between now and then we change the penalty or the minimum age," the government representative explains.

"That doesn't make any sense. It's my money. I should be able to access it whenever I want."

"Well, you can access it whenever you want as long as you're old enough or you pay the penalty."

"And when I invest my money in your plan, I can then make sure it gets invested in anything I want, right?"

"No. You can't invest in anything that we might consider a conflict of interest."

"What do you mean conflict of interest? It's my money."

"A conflict of interest. You can't invest the money if it personally benefits you."

"I can't use my money to benefit me? What if I want to invest it in starting a business?"

"No, ma'am. That's a prohibited transaction."

"But if I invest through a brokerage firm, in the stock market, isn't it benefiting the brokerage and the businesses whose stock I own?"

"Yes, ma'am."

"But I can't invest it in a way that benefits me?"

"That would be a conflict of interest," the representative repeats.

"Okay. Well, I'm an employer. I want to set up a retirement account for me but not my employees. Can I do that?"

"No, ma'am. That's discrimination."

"But it's my money. I pay myself more than I pay my employees, and that's never been a problem."

"That's fine, ma'am, but you can't discriminate with one of our plans."

"Well, at least I know I don't have to take the money out until I'm seventy-two."

"That's true for people who are seventy-two this year, but it may not be true for you."

"Well, what will be true for me?"

"We can't tell you that."

"What do you mean you can't tell me that? You can't tell me how long I can keep my money tax-deferred?"

"We don't know. We'll know when we decide."

"When will you decide?"

"We'll let you know when we decide."

"What about taxes? Can you at least tell me how much I'll have to pay in taxes when the tax-deferral period is over?"

"No, ma'am. We'll tell you that when it's time."

"Can you at least promise me that it won't be higher than it is now?"

"No, ma'am."

"Can you promise me that it won't go above a certain cap, say 40 percent tax rate?"

"No, ma'am."

"Can you promise me that you won't take more than 50 percent of my money in taxes?"

"We can't promise you anything, ma'am."

"So if I invest in your plan, the only promise you make to me is that I won't have to pay taxes on it this year and that it'll be locked up, but you can't tell me how long it'll be locked up, how much of a penalty I'll have to pay if I need it, what I'll be able to invest in, when is the latest I can defer my taxes, or what tax rate I'll have to pay when the deferral period ends?"

"Yes, ma'am. That's correct."

"So why in the world would I invest using your plan?"

That is a very good question.

CHAPTER 3

401(K) AND PROPERTY LAW: IS THE MONEY REALLY YOURS?

"If you haven't found it yet, keep looking. Don't settle. As with all matters of the heart, you'll know when you find it."
—STEVE JOBS

WHEN YOU CONTRIBUTE MONEY TO A 401(K), that money is still yours, right? It belongs to you? We'd like to think so, but what does it really mean to own property? Does having money in a 401(k) endow the same rights in ownership as other property? Let's take a look.

As every first-year law student learns, property ownership comes with a bundle of legal rights—the rights of possession, control, exclusion, enjoyment, and disposition.[1]

These rights are manifest in anything you own. If you purchase a laptop, you have these rights. You have the right of *possession*, meaning you can take it with you when you buy it. You can travel with it, hook it up to your retina-display monitor at home, or take it to work with you. You can *control* it. You get to choose what software to install, which background to display on its screen, and what stickers to put on its cover. You can *exclude* others from using it. If you don't want your friend borrowing it, then you don't have to let him. You can set passwords to keep unknown others from using it.

You have the right to use and *enjoy* it. You can watch movies, edit photos, and create complicated spreadsheets—whatever makes you happy. And you can *dispose* of it however you want. You can sell it at any price you can fetch. You can donate it to a charity or your nephew, who is a poor college student.

---

1. E.g., *In re W.O.L.F.*, 574 B.R. 233, 237 (Bankr. D. Colo. 2017).

You can take it to a shooting range and destroy it. Because you own it, those are your rights.

A violation of one of these rights would ordinarily constitute a tort or a crime.[2] For example, violation of the right to possession, control, or exclusion, depending on the circumstances, could be trespass to chattel (unauthorized borrowing) or conversion (stealing), both torts. This could also constitute the crime of larceny (if stolen), robbery (if taken under force or threat of force), or burglary (if someone broke into your home to take it).

If it is real estate, an interference with your right of enjoyment constitutes nuisance. If someone places an improper lien or lis pendens on your house, interfering with your right of disposition (and preventing you from selling it), that's slander of title, a tort.

Your rights in property are not absolute. There are limitations. If your enjoyment of your laptop includes hitting someone over the head with it, that's obviously not within your rights. So where the rights of your property interfere with others' rights, there are bounds.

There are other legal limits as well. For example, if you purchase a house, you have the right to exclude others from that property. If someone comes onto your property anyway, it becomes a violation called "trespass," which is both a tort and a crime.

There may be legal easements, however, that allow certain others to enter your property, your menacing no-trespassing signs notwithstanding. For example, the city has a right to enter your property to read the power meter. A police officer with a warrant has a right to enter and search the parts of your house covered by a warrant. The mailman can walk up to your door to deliver your mail through the slot in your door. These are established limitations to your right to exclude.

There are other limitations that you voluntarily assume. For example, when you finance a purchase, such as a house or a car, you are not paying for it

---

2. A tort is a civil wrong. It's like the civil equivalent of a crime, though not all torts have a criminal counterpart and vice versa.

with your own money and are relying on others to get it now. As a result, you are going to give up certain rights to get the loan. The bank is going to require you to secure your loan by giving it superior rights to yours if you default on the payments. That way, they can repossess what is yours, make it theirs, and it will all be legal because you've granted them that authority in the contract.

Your right of disposition is also limited when a vehicle is financed. Sure, you can still sell it to whomever you want for whatever price you want, and you could also donate it, but only if you pay off your loan first.

But none of that makes the car any less yours. The bank doesn't tell you where to drive, who your passengers are going to be, to whom you can lend the car, or which presidential candidate's stickers you can slap on your bumper. You still get to make all those decisions.

There are a number of limitations on your property rights that can occur either through legal or voluntary means, but that doesn't change the nature of ownership or how it feels to be the owner. You are still in charge, and the limits are typically insubstantial. It has never been a deal breaker in a real-estate purchase when the buyer finds out that they won't be able to prevent the meter reader from taking electricity usage readings from their new home.

So let's talk about the 401(k) and your bundle of property rights.

The money you're thinking about putting into a 401(k) is yours. It is money that comes from income you've earned from a job. That money has all the rights associated with ownership. You can stick it in your wallet, a piggy bank, or a bank account (possession). You can save it, spend it, invest it, or do origami with it (control). You can keep it for yourself (exclusion). You can use it to purchase admission to a concert, go on vacation, or add to your action-figure collection (enjoyment). Of course, you can donate it, burn it to stay warm, or trade it for Mexican pesos (disposition). What you can do with your money is virtually limitless. Cash is king, as they say.

But once you decide to contribute to a 401(k), what happens? Every dollar you put into that qualified account becomes subject to a new set of rules—a set of rules that infringes on every single one of those property rights.

Possession: You no longer have the money, and you no longer have the right to have the money. It's now likely being held by an investment firm—Fidelity, Charles Schwab, Edward Jones, or the like. It's not in your wallet, in your piggy bank, or your bank account. It's not allowed to be.

Control: You no longer have unlimited control in how you use your money. Your options are limited both by the IRS and by your investment firm. The IRS forbids "prohibited transactions," allowing only certain investments, and in most cases, you're going to be in a mutual fund. Your options are further limited by whatever investment firm is managing your 401(k). They'll ask you a few questions about goals and risk aversion and show you several options for different mutual funds you can choose. That's the extent of your choices. You have very little control over your money now.

Putting your money in a 401(k) is a lot like trading your cash for casino chips. Those chips allow you to buy anything the casino says you can buy, which usually is not much. If you walk out of the casino and try to spend your chips at a gas station, restaurant, or online, you're going to be very disappointed. Nope, those chips are only good inside the casino and only for certain things. You have to trade them back out again for cash when you leave the casino if you want your money to have any buying power.

That's the way it is with the 401(k). When you put your money in, you're basically trading for chips, which means you can now only use that money on the limited investments the 401(k) allows. The difference is, you can't just trade your chips for money at the door—not without a steep penalty. It's like the Hotel California, except you can leave, but you can never check out.

You also don't get to keep it in the 401(k) as long as you want. Perhaps you don't need the money for retirement. Perhaps you are still working and wanting to grow the account more. It doesn't matter. Once you turn seventy-two, the government's patience has run out, and it wants its taxes now—so you have to start withdrawing money and paying taxes.

Exclusion: Here, you don't really have a choice either. Now that your money is in a 401(k), everyone but the investment firm is excluded from using it, including you (unless you want to pay to use your own money. That's where the 10 percent penalty and taxes comes in or the interest you pay to someone else on a loan you make to yourself).

Enjoyment: Because you don't possess the money, have little control over it, and are excluded from it, you do the math as to how much you're actually going to enjoy having that money. Sure, it may have given you some peace of mind knowing you were saving for retirement, but that was before you knew what you were really agreeing to. If you really understand the 401(k), enjoyment is the last thing you're feeling.

Disposition: Here, too, the government gets to choose. You want to cash out of the 401(k)? No problem. Just pay a 10 percent penalty and taxes on the entire sum. Want to pass it to your heirs when you die? That's fine, but they will have to withdraw money on the government's terms. As of January 2020, that means they have to withdraw it all within ten years and pay taxes on 100 percent of the withdrawals at their ordinary income tax rate.

Is the 401(k) money really yours if you can't possess it, control it, are excluded from it, can't enjoy it, and have to dispose of it on the government's terms? Sure, everyone says it's yours. But even if your name is on it, if it doesn't feel like yours and you don't have any of the rights ordinarily associated with ownership, does it really matter? If it walks like a duck and talks like a duck, we can call it a giraffe, but it's still a duck. That 401(k) money is yours in name only.

Which means it isn't really yours at all.

CHAPTER 4

401(K)S AND PUBLIC
V. PRIVATE INVESTING

"If we command our wealth, we shall be rich and free.
If our wealth commands us, we are poor indeed."
—EDMUND BURKE

YOU ARE PROBABLY FAMILIAR WITH THE TERMS "public sector" and "private sector." The public sector is that part of the economy owned and operated by the government. The private sector comprises the rest of us—large corporations, small businesses, babysitters, and paperboys.

The private sector is profit driven. People go into business to make money. In the private sector, if a business is not profitable, it makes changes to become profitable. It must be self-sustaining, meaning it has to produce more money than it spends. If it's unprofitable for too long, it doesn't survive.[1]

In the public sector, profit is not the primary concern. The purpose of the public sector is to provide services to the public, like transportation, electricity, education, and mining. Profitability is not essential. The government can fund or subsidize the public services with taxes—money it takes from its citizens.

Soon-to-be Ghostbuster Ray Stantz made a pithy comparison of the two sectors right after he lost his job as a university professor. He commiserated with Peter Venkman, who had also been fired: "Personally, I like the university. They gave us money and facilities. We didn't have to produce anything. You've never

---

1. Unless the private company is considered "too big to fail," and the government believes it would have too negative an impact on the economy, the government may provide a "bail out." *See* the brief review of basic economics above on page 8.

been out of college. You don't know what it's like out there. I've worked in the private sector. They expect results."[2]

There are countless jokes about the efficiency and profitability of the public v. private sectors, but let's just take a look at one unique case: the United States Postal Service (USPS).

The USPS is in an interesting situation because, although it is a public entity—it is a division of the U.S. Government—it does not receive tax dollars to subsidize it.[3] That means that it is expected to adapt to changing circumstances to remain profitable, but it can't make changes to its business without a literal act of Congress.

Since 2007, the USPS has realized losses in the multiple billions every year. In 2019, their net annual loss was $8.8 billion.[4] And it's no wonder why. We live in a world where envelopes are being replaced by emails, and parcels are being directly delivered by Amazon employees. When they aren't, FedEx and UPS are in the market.

UPS and FedEx are private entities, free to make daily changes to their operations to promote their ultimate goal: profitability. How can the Post Office compete?

Although neither UPS nor FedEx (nor any private entity) is immune to market ups and downs, if USPS were publicly traded, and you were choosing between the USPS, UPS, and FedEx for a place to invest, would the USPS even make the running?

If given the choice, would you ever invest in a public business over its private competition? Not a chance!

---

2. *Ghostbusters*, ©1984.
3. On August 22, 2020, citing concerns about voting fraud associated with a high number of mail-in ballots due to coronavirus-related shutdowns, the House passed a bill that would provide $25B in funding to the Post Office. This is not expected to pass the Senate, but may be a portent for future expenditures (and corresponding tax hikes).
4. USPS, "U.S. Postal Service Reports Fiscal Year 2019 Results," November 14, 2019, last accessed July 8, 2020, https://about.usps.com/newsroom/national-releases/2019/1114-usps-reports-fiscal-year-2019-results.htm. The USPS releases their profit and loss statements every year (and every quarter).

But isn't that exactly what a 401(k) is? It is a government "retirement" plan. It's part of the *tax* code, that set of words that is constantly changing in all but its main purpose: to take money from your pocket and give it to the government. Remember, the 401(k) was born as a result of an amendment to the tax code called "The *Revenue* Act of 1978," as in "a way to generate revenue for the government."

Somewhere, someone in the government is having a good laugh at the fact that the 401(k) is a tax revenue generating tool of the government, has always been labeled "tax" and "revenue," and yet millions of people are still contributing. They don't even realize that they've gambled their entire retirement on a tax-generation vehicle.

> **Somewhere, someone in the government is having a good laugh at the fact that the 401(k) is a tax revenue generating tool of the government, has always been labeled "tax" and "revenue," and yet millions of people are still contributing. They don't even realize that they've gambled their entire retirement on a tax-generation vehicle.**

If that's not enough to convince you that Congress knows the 401(k) is a bad deal for taxpayers, consider this: What are members of Congress doing for their own retirement?

Although most members of Congress are undoubtedly involved in their own private retirement planning, with very few notable exceptions, members of Congress also participate in the congressional pension plan.

Congress's pension plan is set forth in a federal statute called the Federal Employees' Retirement System (FERS).[5] FERS is a defined-benefit program—the same kind of program that employers used to fund that guaranteed a certain

5. 5 U.S.C. § 84.

annual income for pensioned retirees, the same kind of program that the 401(k) replaced when employers realized they could shift the risk and cost of retirement to the employees.[6]

These private pensions are rarer and rarer now because employers can shift the risk and cost of retirement to their employees by sponsoring a 401(k) instead. But why would Congress want to participate in a defined-contribution plan like the 401(k) when they can participate in a defined-benefit plan like FERS? Remember, a 401(k) defines the money going in but makes no guarantee about the money available at the other end (you know, because taxes, investment fees, and market risk). FERS defines the benefits, so legislators know from the outset what their retirement is going to be.

Of course, members of Congress have a huge advantage over you and me. They can pick their retirement plan. They wrote the statute that takes money from taxpayers and puts it into a pension system for them. You and I don't have that option. We can't just take money from others and use it for ourselves, retirement or otherwise. In the private sector, that's called theft.

Ron Paul, a former member of the U.S. House of Representatives (and presidential candidate), called the congressional pension system "immoral" for having "a taxpayer-funded pay-out which is more lucrative than any private system."[7]

Why doesn't Congress create a 401(k) plan for itself? Because it wants taxes to fund its retirement, not its retirement to fund taxes.

Why doesn't Congress create a 401(k) plan for itself? Because it wants taxes to fund its retirement, not its retirement to fund taxes.

6. *See* the discussion starting at page 12.
7. Office of U.S. Representative Ron Paul, "Paul Refuses to Participate in 'Immoral' Pension System," January 30, 1997, last accessed July 8, 2020, http://www.house.gov/paul/press/press97/prjan30.htm (as archived at http://web.archive.org/web/20070518101118/http://www.house.gov/paul/press/press97/prjan30.htm).

CHAPTER 5

401(k)s DURING RETIREMENT

*"When it is obvious that the goals cannot be reached, don't
adjust the goals, adjust the action steps."*
—CONFUCIUS

IF YOU ARE ONE OF the millions of Americans who is investing in a 401(k), let's take a look at what that's going to look like you for you during retirement. After all, isn't that why you contributed to the 401(k) in the first place—for your retirement?

Before we continue, let's remind ourselves what we mean by the word "retirement." For me, that word conjures images of an older silver-haired couple slow dancing on a cruise ship ballroom floor, sipping fancy drinks under an umbrella on the beach, or braving the rain as they explore the sights of an old European city. I also picture them in an RV traveling from state to state, stopping to see the sights, spending a few weeks at a time at each and in no particular hurry. I picture them at home in a modest but upscale ranch-style house restoring old vehicles, woodworking in the garage, gardening, reading, and playing Scrabble.

That may not be the same images everyone else sees when they picture retirement. However, there are several attributes in common among most, if not all, visions of retirement.

First, the retiree is going to have more time on their hands than they did during their working lives. Isn't that the purpose of retirement? To leave the mundane demands of a job behind? To spend time relaxing, doing the things you've always wanted to do but didn't have the time to do? Second, unless the retiree's plan is limited to Netflix and crossword puzzles in a single-wide trailer or living with their adult kids, retirement is going to require far more income than Social Security will provide.

That's really what we're talking about when we talk about retirement in a financial planning sense: money. Income. Income is such a crucial part of our working lives that we switch jobs to make more of it and negotiate the point more than any other when we are on the job hunt. We tie much of our self-worth to how much money we make. But for whatever reason, many of us are not near as concerned about income after we stop working (retirement), when it's so much harder to come by.

RETIREMENT FOR A HIGHER INCOME INDIVIDUAL

Let's imagine a thirty-one-year-old dentist making $250,000 per year, which will increase steadily over the course of her career. We'll call her Dr. A. Because Dr. A is retirement minded, she starts putting away $36,000 every year ($3,000 monthly) starting on her thirty-first birthday. Only $19,500 of that can go into her 401(k) because of the limits the government has set,[1] so she uses the other $16,500 in her day-trading investments.

Dr. A gets a $19,500 tax deduction for money contributed to her 401(k). Since she's in the 35 percent tax bracket, she saves $6,825 in taxes every year. But she's going to have to pay taxes on her day-trading gains. We are going to assume a 5.42 percent annual increase in her investments because from 1896 through the middle of 2018, that's what the average annual Dow Jones return has been.[2]

Now let's assume she does this through age sixty-five, and on her sixty-fifth birthday, she begins her first day of retirement.

---

1. These limits are for unmarried individuals. The limits increase for those who are married. We could just as easily have run this scenario for someone who was married and had both spouses contribute.
2. Roger Wahlner, April 22, 2020, "Average Stock Market Return," Wealthsimple.com, April 22, 2020, last accessed July 8, 2020, https://www.wealthsimple.com/en-us/learn/average-stock-market-return.

Under those assumptions, on day one of retirement, over the last thirty-five years, she will have saved $238,875 in taxes from the 401(k) contribution deductions. But she will have also spent $305,071.88 in taxes on her day trading gains.[3]

Nevertheless, she's still in pretty good shape. Her 401(k) account has a balance of $2,026,544.85, and her day-trading investment account—which she is going to continue to invest through retirement—has $1,165,026.35 in it.

Because Dr. A's annual income increased by 1.15 percent every year, her income was $414,749.09 when she retired.[4]

Dr. A decides that to maintain her standard of living, she wants to withdraw about $23,000 per month. Before celebrating how great a retirement this will be, remember, this is thirty-five years in the future, which means the dollar will not go near as far then as it does now. In fact, if we use the average rate of inflation from 1929 to 2020 of 3.08 percent, we can project that thirty-five years into the future, it will take $4.42 to have the buying power of one dollar today.[5] Yikes. That means $23,000 monthly in thirty-five years will be the equivalent of about $5,203 monthly today. That no longer seems so high.

In her working years, Dr. A had assumed that she would be in a lower tax bracket when she retired. It wasn't anything she actually thought about to any degree—it was just something the experts seemed to agree on.

But remember, Dr. A's tax bracket depends on two things: her taxable income and her deductions. So the only way for Dr. A to be in a lower tax

---

3. Because Dr. A's day trading supplements her ordinary income, it is taxed at the highest bracket she qualifies for. In other words, her ordinary income has already accounted for taxes in all the lower brackets, so income from trading gets taxed at the highest percent of all her brackets. See explanation of bracketed taxes in a progressive system at footnote 7 of this Chapter.
4. For our purposes, it doesn't really matter what her income is at this point except that it sets a bar regarding standard of living. Once she hits $518,400, she gets bumped up to the next tax bracket and starts paying an extra 3% in taxes for everything above that.
5. Kimberly Amedeo and Janet Berry-Johnson, "U.S. Inflation Rate by Year 1929–2022," The Balance, updated July 1, 2020, last accessed July 8, 2020, https://www.thebalance.com/u-s-inflation-rate-history-by-year-and-forecast-3306093.

bracket when she retires is if her taxable income is lower, she has more deductions, or some combination of the two.

The good news is that the $1,165,026.35 from day trading is money Dr. A can use, and it doesn't count as income. She's been paying taxes on that along the way, remember? So the only taxes she has to pay on that money is on the growth she continues to experience through her retirement-years' day trading.

The bad news is that the $2,026,544.85 in her 401(k) is taxable, 100 percent. If she is going to use $23,000 per month, that puts her in the 35 percent tax bracket, which is the tax bracket she was in when she was working. (Of course, if taxes go up in the future, as most people believe, then that rate will be higher.)

So now Dr. A starts to look at what deductions she can use to decrease her income into a lower tax bracket.

The deductions that were most beneficial to Dr. A when she was working were the ones from her dependent children, her business-related expenses, the mortgage interest payments, and the student-loan interest payments. But she realizes that none of these deductions apply to her anymore. Her children are grown and are no longer dependents. She is no longer practicing dentistry, so she doesn't get the business-related deductions. And her mortgage and student loans are paid off. The standard deduction for single filers is $12,400, and that may be all she gets.[6]

Dr. A realizes that she is not in a lower tax bracket after all. Then it dawns on her: if she has to pay up to 35 percent of the 401(k) withdrawals in taxes, and she needs $23,000 *after* taxes, that means she actually has to withdraw much more than $23,000.[7]

---

6. Again, we're assuming things don't change between now and retirement, even though they will, and they're likely to get worse.

7. Because ours is a progressive or graduated tax system, your tax bracket defines the highest tax rate you pay on all the income above the threshold of the tax bracket. You don't pay that rate on all your income. For example, if you are in the 22% tax bracket for 2020, that means you make at least $40,126 but no more than $85,525 (for a single person). If you make $60,126 in taxable income, then you only pay 22% on the last $20,000 of your income (the $20,000 in that bracket). The first $40,126 gets taxed at lower rates corresponding with the ranges defined by the tax brackets. For purposes of our math, we are calculating 35% on the whole, which assumes that we are still using a progressive system in the future, that taxes have gone up, and that the average graduated rate of your taxes is 35%, which in our estimate is pretty conservative.

Dr. A decides she is going to take a portion of her monthly income out of the 401(k) and part of it out of the day-trading account. She only has to pay taxes on the growth of the day-trading account, but she has to pay taxes on all of the money from the 401(k).

She figures out that she needs to withdraw $18,333.33 per month from her 401(k) and $10,416.67 from her day-trading account. Because that account is still growing by 5.42 percent annually, she still will have to pay those taxes too. So Dr. A has to pay taxes on all of the 401(k) she withdraws, none of the day-trading she withdraws, but she will have to pay taxes on the growth in the investment account. That means between the two, she'll have withdrawn $28,750 per month and sent $5,578.69 to the IRS, leaving her with $23,171.31.

Both the day-trading account and 401(k) are still growing by 5.42 percent annually, but Dr. A's retirement account is still shrinking because of her retirement withdrawals.

At this rate, under this scenario, Dr. A's retirement will last just over twelve years. As she is celebrating her seventy-seventh half-birthday, her money will be gone. At seventy-seven, Dr. A finds a new appreciation for crossword puzzles, which she can more than afford on her Social Security income, which is all she has left.

That's kind of bleak. We'll call that Scenario A. So let's change some of the facts and assume that Dr. A's employer matches her 401(k) contributions, up to $6,000 annually. Further, let's assume that instead of being a day trader, she is investing in long-term mutual funds (holding them for at least a year), which means she is not paying the income tax rate, just the capital gains rate of 15 percent.

Let's see how those numbers shake out:

	Scenario A	Scenario A with Employer Matching
Total Invested at 65	$1,260,000.00	$1,470,000.00
Total Growth at 65	$1,931,571.20	$2,629,014.60
Total Accumulated at 65	$3,191,571.20	$4,099,014.60
Total Taxes Paid in Retirement	$1,350,843.71	$1,408,696.54
Years before Money Runs Out	12.5	16.9

Those two changes make a big difference, giving her an extra $900,000 of retirement and extending her retirement out by another 4.4 years.

Now let's inject a little dose of reality into the scenario. We've made some assumptions that simply won't hold up for the next thirty-five years. And they're going to make a significant difference in the outcome. Let's just look at four of those assumptions:

- that the growth will be a constant 5.42 percent rather than an average of several ups and downs
- that there were no fees associated with the investment account that would slow growth
- that Dr. A will not need long-term care
- that taxes will be the same in the future as they are now and will not increase

Let's discuss each of those and explore how each would affect the outcome.

Constant (Average) Versus Fluctuating Returns

When we talk of average returns, we understand what that means. We know from grade school that if Amar scores an eight on his quiz, Andaluz scores nine, and Billy gets a seven, their average score is eight. Using the same math (adding up all the scores and dividing by the number of scores), we can calculate the average rate of return for the Dow Jones Industrial Average from 1896 through May 2018: 5.42 percent average growth.

But getting a constant 5.42 percent growth year after year for 122 years gets you an entirely different result than if your growth and loss fluctuates every year and merely averages out to be 5.42 percent.

Consider this example. Let's say that on day one, a stock goes up by 50 percent. Then on day two, it goes down by 50 percent. The average rate of return over those two days is zero percent, right? ([-50 + 50]/2 = 0.) So you might expect that if you invested at the beginning of day one, and you sold at the end of day two, then you would have the same amount you started with, right?

Wrong.

The problem with thinking that way is that the numbers change between day one and day two. The market change has an effect on what you invest, and so the first percentage and the second percentage are affecting different amounts of money.

Let's look at it this way: If you invested one hundred dollars in the stock on day one, and experienced 50 percent growth, you are now at $150. Then, when you experience 50 percent loss, that's 50 percent of $150, not 50 percent of one hundred dollars. So now you're at seventy-five dollars. So even though the market has averaged no gains and no losses, you are down 25 percent.

What if the stock market goes down by 50 percent first and then up by 50 percent? Your one hundred dollars from day one turns into fifty dollars (50 percent drop) and then seventy-five dollars (50 percent increase). So you are still down 25 percent.

Why is that? When the market's average is flat, why do you lose money regardless of whether the growth or loss comes first? It's based on a very simple principle that you can observe when you look at the curves on the market-fluc-tuation graph. **When the market changes, your percentage loss is always on the high number and your percentage gain is always on the low number:**

This is the Dow Jones Industrial Average for a single day: April 23, 2020. Google populates this chart based on the day's returns when you enter "Dow Jones Industrial Average" in Google's search bar.

That's a pretty scary phenomenon, but only if you are relying on averages (which we do all the time). In this graph, you can see that the average daily increase was 0.53 percent. But that doesn't mean if you invested first thing and sold when the average was 0.53 percent higher that your investment would be 0.53 percent higher. Your money had to go through the ridges and valleys first to get to the average.

So what does that mean for our retirement example? Well, we took the average stock market increase over time and used that to calculate growth. But the reality is, since the nineteenth century, on average, the stock market corrects by 43 percent every 9.875 years. [8]

---

8. I calculated both of these averages by taking every major stock market downturn in the last 100+ years.

Timing then becomes very important. A stock market correction like that in your early years is something you can recover from. But what if it is something that happens right before, or worse, after your retirement begins? That would completely wipe out years of your savings. Let's face it, if they happen on average every 9.875 years, it's probably going to happen right before or during your retirement at least once.

If instead of using a flat 5.42 percent growth every year, we instead assume ten to eleven percent gains year over year with 35 percent in losses every nine years, keeping our average of 5.42 percent, things look quite a bit different:

	Scenario A Flat 5.42%	Scenario A Fluctuating Rates Average 5.42%
Total Invested at 65	$1,260,000.00	$1,260,000.00
Total Growth at 65	$1,931,571.20	$ 742,877.15
Total Accumulated at 65	$3,191,571.20	$2,002,877.15
Total Taxes Paid in Retirement	$1,350,843.71	$ 344,276.38
Years before Money Runs Out	12.5	8.92

In fact, even though we've invested the same amount of money over the same amount of time and experienced the same average rate of return, we've effectively cut over 3.5 years off (28.6 percent) of Dr. A's retirement!

The biggest problem with these facts is that you can't control them. You have no power over when the market corrects. You can't change the math and make it so you can earn on the big numbers and take losses on the small ones. If you choose to put your retirement in a vehicle attached to the stock market, that's a reality you have to face.

Don't forget, that money in your 401(k), it's income. Future income. It will form a very important part of your future. Why are we putting our income—something we rely on to survive—in something as volatile as the stock market?

During your working years, if your employer offered to put your entire paycheck into the stock market where it would have to sit for a time before you could cash it—and then you'd end up with whatever new amount the stock market dictated—would you do that? No way! You have bills to pay! That money is too important to risk. So why are you doing it with your future income? Paychecks will be much harder to come by when you're not working, so it doesn't make sense to gamble your future paycheck.

The market volatility you risk doesn't even take into account additional losses to your income resulting, not from periodic dips in the stock market but from constant and regular fees being taken from your investments.

Investment Fees

You are probably unaware of all the fees being charged when you create a 401(k). That investment firm that is handling your money? How do you think they make their money? How are those financial advisors earning a living? It's from the fees charged for handling your funds.

This phenomenon—the loss in earning power due to fees and costs of investing—is something called "performance drag." That growth curve you experience when you participate in interest compounding is flattened with performance drag, which causes your growth to slow (or to stop altogether) or your investment performance to, well, drag.

Some of those fees and costs are disclosed and quantified. Some are not. We'll talk specifically about six of them: the expense ratio, investment advisory fee, transaction fees, front-end load, back-end load, and annual account fee.

Expense ratio: The expense ratio is basically the operating and administration expenses for your plan. It is expressed in a percentage and usually ranges from .05 percent to upwards of 2 percent. The average expense ratio is between

0.5 percent and 1 percent. A 1 percent expense ratio means that for every one hundred dollars you invest, one dollar will go to the brokerage firm. The law requires these fees to be disclosed.

Investment Advisory Fees: This is a percentage charged, usually on a quarterly basis, of the total money under management. This is also expressed as a percentage and is usually between 1 percent and 2 percent. So for every one hundred dollars, they will take one dollar per year, usually paid quarterly, so it would be twenty-five cents every quarter. This is not just on new money invested but total money under management. So if you have $100,000 invested in year one that increases to $110,000 in year two, the investment advisory fee at 1.5 percent will be $1,500 in year one and $1,650 in year two.

Transaction Fees: These are per-transaction flat fees. Every time you want to make a trade (buy or sell a stock), they'll charge you a transaction fee. Those typically range from ten dollars to over fifty dollars per trade. Charles Schwab recently made headlines when it announced it would no longer be charging transaction fees for trades on its platform. Several brokers followed suit, though the majority still charge a fee for transactions.

But that's not the end of the story. Even when you and I don't engage in transactions, the mutual fund, which consists of a multitude of stocks and bonds, could be trading regularly. Those trades cause the broker to incur transaction fees, which gets passed onto you.

Front-end Load: The front-end load is a sales commission charged to establish your mutual fund. Front-end loads typically cost between 3.75 percent to 5.75 percent of the investment amount. This is typically going to be graduated, so the more you invest, the lower the fee gets. If you invest $700,000, that may entitle you to a discounted front-end load of "only" 2 percent ($14,000), whereas if you are only investing $40,000, you may pay a 4.25 percent front-end load ($1,700). Some investment firms charge a flat rate. If you stick $10,000 in a mutual fund, and there is a 4.5 percent front-end load, that means your investment advisor is going to get the first $450, and the value of your mutual fund on day one is actually going to be $9,550. This means you have to get a 4.7 percent return before you're back where you started.

Back-end Load or Surrender Charge: The same mutual fund will likely only have either a front-end load or a back-end load, not both. Whereas the front-end charge is incurred when the fund is purchased, the back-end charge/surrender charge is incurred when you sell your fund. Usually, the longer you own the fund before you sell it, the lower your back-end load will be. A typical back-end load is going to be 5 percent for the first year, and then one percentage point lower for each subsequent year you own the fund before you sell. This fund is to make sure the brokerage firm and agent still make money even if they don't manage your fund for very long.

Annual Account Fee (Custodian Fee): This is a flat annual fee the broker will charge. If they are handling a qualified account, like a 401(k), they are required to report the balance and growth of your fund to the IRS every year, and they charge for that. The annual account fee will usually range between twenty-five dollars and one hundred dollars.

These are not the only costs associated with these mutual funds. Cash drag also contributes to performance drag. Cash drag relates to the realities of conducting a business. The broker you've invested with has to have cash on hand. Just like other businesses, cash is required to pay employees, use for emergencies, and keep liquid for when investors want to cash out or to use for better timing of investments, etc. Unfortunately, though, when part of your money is kept in cash, it is not earning and not even keeping up with inflation, causing negative growth. If a firm keeps 10 percent of its money under management in cash, then only 90 percent of your money is working for you.

Another contributor to performance drag is tax drag—the losses to growth you incur when your principal shrinks due to taxes. A big part of the reason you stuck your money in a 401(k) was so the growth you experience would be uninterrupted by tax payments. It's a tax-deferred vehicle, remember?

That's true, so you're not going to have to pay tax on the growth until you withdraw it, but the same isn't true for your investment broker. Your money is locked away to you, but your broker is still making money on it—in the form of all these fees. Your broker does have to pay taxes every year on its profit. Where do you think the money comes from to pay the broker's taxes? **It comes from you.**

All of the investment fees have a devastating effect on your 401(k).

All of the investment fees have a devastating effect on your 401(k). Taken together, Forbes estimated in 2011 that the real cost of owning a mutual fund is between 3.17 percent and 4.17 percent annually.[9] In a more recent analysis, Forbes estimated the growth erosion to be as much as 6.22 percent off the percentage growth of your mutual fund. This means that if the market grew by 8 percent, you may only experience 1.78 percent growth after all the known and hidden costs, and your losses are compounded if the stock market drops.[10]

Let's return to Dr. A, the dentist. Remember, she is contributing the maximum $19,500 per year to her 401(k) and another $16,500 through private investments every year from age thirty-one through age sixty-five. She is experiencing an average 5.42 percent growth on all her investments. We've already looked at what happens when we calculate steady growth versus fluctuating growth with the same average. Now let's see how investment costs might affect the growth.

We'll assume a modest 2 percent in annual fees:

---

9. "The Real Cost of Owning a Mutual Fund," Forbes.com, April 4, 2011, last accessed July 8, 2020, https://www.forbes.com/2011/04/04/real-cost-mutual-fund-taxes-fees-retirement-bernicke.html.
10. Kenneth Kim, "How Much Do Mutual Funds Really Cost?" Forbes.com, September 24, 2016, last accessed April 23, 2020, https://www.forbes.com/sites/kennethkim/2016/09/24/how-much-do-mutual-funds-really-cost.

	Scenario A Flat 5.42%	Scenario A Flat 5.42% with 2% Annual Fees
Total Invested at 65	$1,260,000.00	$1,260,000.00
Total Growth at 65	$1,931,571.20	$953,057.60
Total Accumulated at 65	$3,191,571.20	$2,213,057.60
Total Taxes Paid in Retirement	$1,350,843.71	$360,955.37
Years before Money Runs Out	12.5	9.98

This simple change, reflected in the reality of mutual fund fees and costs, reduces Dr. A's total retirement savings by a fifth and cuts $2^1/_2$ years off the life of her retirement.

If we apply the same math to the scenario with fluctuating rates rather than a constant 5.42 percent, the results are even more bleak:

	Scenario A Flat 5.42% with 2% Annual Fees	Scenario A Fluctuating Rates Average 5.42% with 2% Annual Fees
Total Invested at 65	$1,260,000.00	$1,260,000.00
Total Growth at 65	$953,057.600	$122,113.03
Total Accumulated at 65	$2,213,057.60	$1,382,113.03
Total Taxes Paid in Retirement	$360,955.37	$164,214.94
Years before Money Runs Out	9.98	7.15

Now Dr. A only has 7.15 years of retirement. What's really alarming is that over thirty-five years of saving, her account has only grown by $122,113.03, which is less than she's going to pay in taxes during retirement!

Of course, at this point, if Dr. A is already retired when she realizes this, she is going to change her plans and figure out how to make do with much less than $23,000 per month. And if she hasn't retired yet, she's thinking twice about putting any more money into a 401(k).

Long-term Care Expenses

Another assumption we made was that Dr. A wouldn't need long-term care and that she would never get any sort of chronic or terminal illness that might require dedicated medical care.

This is not really something Dr. A can bet on though. Morning Star, an independent investment research firm, estimates that 52 percent of all people turning sixty-five will need some sort of long-term care in their lifetime.[11] The average long-term care need is 2.5 years for women and 1.5 years for men.[12] The median annual cost ranges from $18,200 to $215,770, depending on whether it is in-home adult day care, an assisted-living facility, or nursing home. Private rooms are more expensive, and if you're in Manhattan, you're paying top dollar.

That means, on average, those who need long-term care will need somewhere between $27,300 and $539,425. That's a huge range and potentially a huge chunk out of your finite retirement fund.

We don't need to do the inflation math to figure out that if you are one of the 52 percent who needs some sort of long-term care, that's going to put a significant dent in your retirement. Every dent has a ripple effect on the future of your retirement fund in the form of lost investment growth through principal depletion.

---

11. Christine Benz, Aug 20, 2018, "75 Must-Know Statistics About Long-Term Care: 2018 Edition," https://www.morningstar.com/articles/879494/75-must-know-statistics-about-long-term-care-2018-edition, last accessed July 8, 2020.
12. *Id.*

Tax Changes

We have already discussed the state of flux of the tax code and how taxes have frequently changed over time. And this code will continue to change. But have you thought about the impact this will have on your retirement account? If 2 percent in investment fees has such a significant impact on your retirement lifestyle, what will the effect be if taxes go up by 10 percent?

During the last several decades, we have experienced the lowest tax rates in history, yet we've run up the national debt through a consistent ginormous deficit. Consequently, taxes really have only one direction to go: up.[13] Way up.

> ### Qualified plans, like the 401(k), are essentially an annuity for the government that you're funding.

Qualified plans, like the 401(k), are essentially an annuity for the government that you're funding. With an annuity, you can make regular and periodic payments for a certain period of time. Then once the annuity matures, you have a guaranteed income for life. That's possible because the insurance company selling you the annuity is taking your money and pooling it with other money to go make large investments and make money. That works because you are giving them enough time to make money and still guarantee you a monthly lifetime income.

Isn't that what the government is doing with you? They are making regular and periodic payments (by collecting fewer taxes when you make contributions) for a certain period of time (your working years). Then once the annuity matures (you retire), the government has a guaranteed income for life (taxes on everything in your account).

There are at least two major differences, though. First, unlike the insurance company, you aren't pooling your money and making huge returns. You're handing your money over to a broker who is making money off your

---

13. *See* the discussion of historical tax rates at pages 6–8, which shows how much higher taxes were for most of the twentieth century.

money. But you're still the one who has to fund the government's annuity once it matures.

Second, with an actual annuity, you and the insurance company reach an agreement as to how much is going to be put in and how much of a lifetime monthly guarantee that will provide. With your government annuity, they get to choose later what that amount will be. That would be like if you could go to the insurance company, make payments toward an annuity, and then when it came time for them to pay you, you get to choose what the monthly amount is going to be. Seems like a great deal, right? Well, it would be, but we don't have that option. Only the government has that privilege.

Here's something else you have to take into account if you are in one of the forty-three states that have income tax: Our scenarios assumed no state income tax. So your retirement could to be depleted by another 5 percent or so (per year—which losses compound over time), depending on what state you retire in. Taxes are the single biggest killer of your qualified retirement income.

Taxes are the single biggest killer of your qualified retirement income.

Social Security

You might be thinking that even if things don't turn out the way you hope with your 401(k), at least you can count on your Social Security to supplement your income. If that's what you're thinking, I have some bad news for you.

Have you ever heard of a Ponzi scheme? Named for Carlo Pietro Giovanni Guglielmo Tebaldo Ponzi, an Italian conman, a Ponzi scheme is a type of fraud where the perpetrators of the fraud convince investors to put their money in some illegitimate high-return investment scenario.[14] Then with new money from the second wave of investors, the perpetrators pay the first investors (and

---

14. Sometimes the investment is originally legitimate, but it turns into fraud when things go bad with the investments.

themselves). These first investors are so amazed at their returns that they keep their original money in the "investment," maybe put more money in, and tell their friends about it. More and more investors invest, and each new generation of investors is funding previous generations (with more to the perpetrators). Everyone is happy—until the perpetrators can't find enough new money, and the bottom drops out.[15]

That's exactly what our Social Security system is. The money you pay into taxes is not going to a general fund that will grow so the returns will eventually help fund your retirement. Instead your money is going to the government, and it is immediately being given to a retiree who has qualified for Social Security.

In other words, you aren't involved in a legitimate investment. You're just part of the newest wave of investors contributing to the past investors. Since the U.S. population growth continues to slow,[16] there are fewer and fewer taxpayers to fund previous generations,[17] and in particular, the baby boomers.

The U.S. Government has long recognized the impending Social Security implosion. To help offset that, they started taxing you on your Social Security income.

Even though you've been paying a Social Security tax on a lifetime worth of income, it doesn't seem fair that you would be taxed on what amounts to a tax refund during retirement. But you are. It may not be fair, but that's how it is. That's one of those changes to taxes the government made that you could not predict or control. And it happened in 1984—amidst all the other tax changes that reduced income tax now. The piper always has to be paid.

---

15. I have been involved in litigation (as a litigating lawyer) with a number of these Ponzi schemes. They always look legit, and they hook even savvy investors. And they always end the same way.

16. Sandra Leigh Johnson, "Drops in Natural Increase, Net International Migration Resulted in 0.5% Annual Growth to 328.2M," U.S. Census, December 30, 2019, last accessed May 18, 2020, https://www.census.gov/library/stories/2019/12/new-estimates-show-us-population-growth-continues-to-slow.html.

17. Mike Stobbe, "US Births Fall, and Virus Could Drive Them Down More," AP News, May 19, 2020, last accessed May 20, 2020, https://apnews.com/8f871bc2cbe89b72e9e-b01a21ebddb5b.

So here's how it works: as long as your taxable retirement income is less than $25,000 (for single filers) or $32,000 (for married joint filers)—you don't have to pay tax on your Social Security income.

But if your taxable income is above those thresholds, you are going to pay taxes on part of your Social Security income at your highest income tax bracket.

You'll get taxed on **up to 50 percent** (50 percent!)[18] of your Social Security benefits once you start taking home more than $25,000 per year.[19] It gets worse. If you have more than $34,000 (individual) or $44,000 (married) in taxable income, then **up to 85 percent** (85 percent) of your Social Security income is taxed.

The only way to avoid this is to reduce your taxable income at retirement. This means you're going to have to take a lot less out of your 401(k) and have a terrible retirement. Of course, it's not worth it to do that to avoid paying taxes on what will end up being a modest Social Security income. So most will just accept the tax hit and pay it. The only other alternative is to plan ahead so that the money funding your retirement lifestyle is not taxable and does not affect how much Social Security is taxed.

Medicare

What about health insurance? You'll no longer be working during retirement, so you aren't going to be part of your employer's group plan. But you'll qualify for Medicare, so you don't have to worry about that, right? Well, kind of.

---

18. I can't help but recall a scene from one of my favorite movies, *The Princess Bride*. Count Tyrone Rugen is an expert on torture and is researching the effects of his life-sucking machine on the protagonist, the Dread Pirate Roberts. After using the machine on the lowest setting of "1," he tells the pirate, who is semiconscious and incoherent in his pain, "I've just sucked one year of your life away. I might one day go as high as five, but I really don't know what that would do to you." Later in the movie, an enraged Prince Humperdinck sets the machine to its highest setting, "50," and turns it on. Count Rugen, despite his affinity for torture, recognizes the danger and exclaims, in our hero's defense: "Not to 50!" You might say the same thing about this ridiculous Social Security tax where 50 and 85 are the norm.

19. "How Is Social Security Taxed?" AARP Social Security Resource Center, updated April 15, 2020, last accessed May 7, 2020, https://www.aarp.org/retirement/social-security/questions-answers/how-is-ss-taxed/.

Medicare Part A, which is hospital coverage, is something most people will qualify for, and it is not affected by your retirement income. If you qualify for Social Security, you qualify for Part A coverage. And there are other ways to qualify too.

Medicare Part B, which covers outpatient medical care, and Part D, which covers prescription costs, are something you have to pay for. Your premium amounts are based on your taxable income.

The good news is the thresholds are much higher than they are for Social Security, and these premiums are relatively low. The bad news is that the more you have in taxable income, the more you pay in premiums for both B and D.

As of 2020, if you have $87,000 or less (single) or $174,000 (married) in income, you pay the standard monthly premium of $144.60 for Part B.[20] Above $87,000/$174,000, the premiums increase to $202.40 per month. The premiums continue to increase with income increases, up to a maximum of $491.80 per person per month.

For Part D, your premiums increase incrementally based on your income from $12.40 per month to $77.40 per month (on top of the base premium).[21]

401(K) IN RETIREMENT — SUMMARY

The one common theme you should be picking up on when it comes to investing in a 401(k) is lack of control. Once the money goes in, you can't control where it gets invested beyond being able to pick from a handful of different funds. You can't control market fluctuations that can wreak havoc on your future income.

---

20. "Part B Costs," Medicare.gov, last accessed May 7, 2020, https://www.medicare.gov/your-medicare-costs/part-b-costs.
21. "How Income Affects Your Medicare Prescription Drug Coverage Premiums," Medicare.gov, revised June 2019, last accessed May 28, 2020, https://www.medicare.gov/Pubs/pdf/11469-income-affects-drug-premiums.pdf.

You can't control broker fees or the resulting performance drag. You can't control whether you will need future care. You can't control the cost of that care. And you can't control changes in the tax code.

In short, when you put your money in a 401(k), you are tossing cash into a whirlwind, hoping that at some point in the storm, you can pull enough back out to continue living even when you aren't working.

> *When you put your money in a 401(k), you are tossing cash into a whirlwind, hoping that at some point in the storm, you can pull enough back out to continue living even when you aren't working.*

We also know that the money you withdraw from your 401(k) during retirement counts against you. It counts against you for tax purposes, and it can put a significant dent in your Social Security income. It also has the potential of increasing the cost of Medicare.

This is not information you should have to buy a book to get. The government should tell you instead of hiding the rules in thousands of unintelligible words. Your investment advisor should have told you instead of promoting the virtues without disclosing the costs. The sad truth is, you've been hoodwinked. You've been shackled by your own ignorance. But now you know better. So what are you going to do about it?

The best way to maintain control over your investments, and your future, is to not give it up in the first place. But even if you have, it's (almost) never too late to course correct.

CHAPTER 6

THE ROTH IRA

"A good plan violently executed now is better than a perfect plan executed next week."

—George S. Patton

SO FAR, WE HAVE USED THE 401(K) as the poster child for all of the different options you have with qualified accounts: the IRA, SEP, 529, 457(b), etc.—all representing different divisions of the tax code designed to generate revenue for the government. But what about the Roth IRA?

The Roth IRA is a whole different animal and does not share very many attributes with its more diabolical cousins, the qualified plans.

Roth IRAs are relatively new to the scene, having been born from the Taxpayer Relief Act of 1997. Although Congress had gotten better at marketing their tax amendments ("Tax Relief Act" sounds a lot better to the taxpayer than "Revenue Act"), at the end of the day, the tax code really only has one job: take money from your pocket and put it into government coffers.

The original plan, proposed by Senator William Roth (Republican-Delaware), was to bring back the traditional IRA, which was unrecognizable after changes to it in the Tax Reform Act of 1986 under Reagan.

This proposal was stymied by congressional budget rules, which recognized that opening back up the IRA would result in an instant budget shortfall from the immediate deductions people would take.[1] As part of the solution to that problem, Senator Roth introduced Roth IRAs that would allow after-tax contributions. This meant the government could get its money now for those contributing to the Roth IRA and get its money later from the more traditional IRAs.

---

1. Deborah L. Jacobs, "Why—And How—Congress Should Curb Roth IRAs," Forbes.com, March 26, 2012, last accessed July 8, 2020, https://www.forbes.com/sites/deborahljacobs/2012/03/26/why-and-how-congress-should-curb-roth-iras.

As it happens, then, the Roth IRA was an afterthought—a creative solution for a shortfall in the tax budget.

It is unlikely that at the time, Congress appreciated the full scope of what they were doing (a common theme among our lawmakers). What resulted from an attempt to restore the moneymaking IRA without too much upfront costs was arguably the best government-sponsored plan ever created. (Don't get too excited; the bar is pretty low.)

With the Roth IRA, you can contribute after-tax dollars. Like other IRAs, it is then invested, usually in mutual funds, and is allowed to grow—not tax-deferred like other qualified plans—but completely tax free.

Thus, the Roth IRA does not suffer from some of the major drawbacks of other qualified plans.

Although you don't get a deduction for Roth contributions, here's what you do get:

- tax-free growth
- liquidity of contributions
- no required minimum distributions

That's huge. In fact, due to the government's shortsightedness in creating Roths, economists estimated future losses in the billions of dollars in tax-related revenue.[2]

So what's the downside? Unfortunately, the tax legislators did have the foresight to limit their use.

For one thing, the maximum anyone can contribute to a Roth IRA in a given year is severely limited at $6,000 (under the current code), with another $1,000 if you are over fifty.[3] That's never going to be enough to retire on, so a Roth IRA at best is only going to be a slice in your overall retirement pie.

---

2. *Id.*

3. These amounts typically increase a few hundred dollars at a time as the tax code is changed.

Additionally, if you make more than $124,000 (single) or $196,000 (married filing jointly), the amount you can contribute begins to phase out. At $139,000 (single) and $206,000 (married), you are disqualified from contributing at all. It's almost as though the government set it up so that once you can afford to regularly contribute, you are disqualified from doing so.

Moreover, although the money you contribute to a Roth IRA is liquid, the earnings are not. Your earnings are required to stay in the Roth until you are 59½, subject to a 10 percent early withdrawal penalty.

Additionally, if you are investing in mutual funds through your Roth, which you probably are, then you are subjected to the same investment fees that plague the 401(k) and other qualified plans.

Still, on the whole, even if not available to everyone, and certainly lacking the heft to fund your total retirement, Roth IRAs are a far better place to keep your money than a 401(k), IRA, or other qualified account.

PART II

HOW YOUR FINANCIAL PROFESSIONALS MAY BE YOUR BIGGEST LIABILITY

CHAPTER 7

THE FINANCIAL PROFESSIONALS WE HIRE

"When a fellow says it ain't the money but the principle of the thing, it's the money."

— ARTEMAS WARD

AFTER COMPLETING THIRTEEN YEARS of compulsory education, you should have been ready to enter the workforce, and even if not ready for a specialized trade, at least savvy about the basics necessary for your entrance into the world that educated you. But unfortunately, public education leaves us almost entirely bereft of the essential skills that *everyone* could benefit from in favor of more specialized, and even esoteric subjects. These essential skills include practical knowledge about investing, finance, banking, and taxes. We'll call them "money skills."

Mathematics, social studies, science, and English are important. But as part of mathematics, why are we teaching algebra, geometry, and trigonometry but not balancing a budget? In social studies, why do we teach about the Boston Massacre and Boston Tea Party and the famous, "no taxation without representation," but then leave out completely the history of taxation since? Why do we teach the (very) basics of supply and demand, but we omit lessons on investing, banking, and taxes?

Why aren't these money skills part of the required curriculum? Why do we teach knowledge and trades designed to help students earn money from their labors (one of the least efficient ways to earn money), but we don't teach what they need to know to earn money from their money (one of the most efficient)? Or how to manage money so it stretches further? Or what they need to know to keep more of this hard-earned money?

My daughter's high school catalog offers courses that are not atypical for high schools, and it reveals just how backwards our education is. We do not offer very many courses that teach skills that all (or at least most) students could benefit from taking. Instead, as typified by the course offerings from my daughter's high school, we focus on courses that will apply to very few students:[1]

- forensic science: three years offered

- furniture and cabinet making: four years offered

- sports medicine: two years offered

- photography: four years offered

- video production: four years offered

- web design and development: two years offered

- tech theater: two years offered

- ceramics: three years offered

If you are one of the few students who wants to become a carpenter, photographer, or pottery maker, you can start to learn a skill that will be helpful to you in the future. If you are someone who wants to own a business (including carpentry, photography, or pottery), become wealthy, and have a healthy retirement (which should be most everyone), your pickings are much slimmer.

I found two sets of courses in the catalog that do tend toward practical application and would become valuable to almost any graduate who falls outside of the normal standard curriculum (and which were not offered when I was in school): Math of Personal Finance, a one-year course, and Principles of Business and Marketing, a one-year course (followed by three years of progressively advanced marketing courses).

---

1. I reviewed the Desert Oasis Diamondbacks 2017–2018 Course Catalog available at https://stempathways.epscorspo.nevada.edu/wp-content/uploads/2017/11/Line91-DesertOasisCourseCatalog.pdf, last accessed April 27, 2020.

As important as these subjects are, at least at my daughter's school, they are electives, which means not everyone will take these classes. Although I don't know the enrollment numbers in the courses, I do know that the students get to choose to be a part of a crime lab, video production team, cabinetry shop, band, choir, debate team, cheerleading squad, or sports team. With all those much "cooler" choices, how many of them are actually selecting to learn about business or finance?

Moreover, when there are required and elective (i.e., optional) courses, what does this label tell the students about the relative importance of the course? If Business and Math of Personal Finance are in the same category as Ceramics and Mythology and Folklore, and somewhere below the level of importance of learning the capital of Denmark or dissecting a frog—both of which are in classes they are required to take—how much weight are the students going to give these classes?

We don't have to scrutinize the course offerings of a single school for you to know that our public schools aren't teaching some of the most important life skills, these money skills. Just think back to your own experience. Who taught you how to balance your budget, to invest, and to plan for and pay taxes? Who taught you how banks work? How to plan for retirement? Whatever you learned, if you learned it at all, chances are you learned at least some of it wrong (and probably most of it). And you likely didn't learn it in school.

For whatever reason, our education system leaves these subjects to us to learn on our own. We either need to learn outside of public school while we are young, or we need to choose to learn it during our secondary education—usually only if that's our chosen profession.

My parents did not teach me much about budgeting, finance, taxes, and retirement—not because they weren't good parents, but because they didn't know much about it themselves. Money Skills was not a class they were offered growing up, either.

What I have learned about these critically important subjects, I didn't learn in school at all. In fact, I went through public schools in three different states while growing up, took all the general education and field-specific courses to earn an undergraduate degree, and then made it through law school without ever learning these things.

I took two courses on the Constitution, a course on business entities, at least one course on economics, and countless history and math courses. But I learned next to nothing about money skills.

My wife, who of a necessity learned how to budget during her enrollment in the school of hard knocks, was dismayed to learn how much I had racked up in student loan debt while attending the most affordable private university in the country.[2] With her help, we were able to make paying off those loans a priority. However, we knew we couldn't start saving for retirement until we paid off that debt—a lesson we learned from a famous southern radio financial guru. Except we were wrong about that, too. We could have saved for retirement and paid off our debt sooner without spending any more money on debt—but that was a lesson I wouldn't learn until much later.

And that's exactly the gap most of us fall in—that big wide-open space between getting an education and actually having those money skills. So on whom do we rely to help us with personal finance, investments, banking, and taxes? The professionals who have specialized education in money skills.

The problem is, although many professionals profess to understand money, most of them do not. Even if they do have a firm understanding of their respective spheres, that's never going to be enough.

Although many professionals profess to understand money, most of them do not. Even if they do have a firm understanding of their respective spheres, that's never going to be enough.

2. Forbes ranked Brigham Young University as the best education for your money in 2019. (BYU has been getting similarly ranked for its quality of education for the price since I was a student there long ago). Caroline Howard, "America's Best Value Colleges 2019," April 24, 2019, last accessed April 27, 2020, https://www.forbes.com/best-value-colleges.

Consider for a moment that when it comes to money, there are really only two things that matter: (1) earning it and (2) keeping as much of it as we can. And that's where we seek advice from professionals. In the first category, we may seek advice on how to build a resume, how to negotiate a salary, the best ways to market ourselves and our businesses, etc.—questions aimed at earning more money.

But the far more interesting question is, once we earn it, how can we keep as much of our money as possible?

The professionals we rely on to answer this question fall into one of three categories:

1. They're going to tell us where to invest our money to see the best *growth* (financial planners).

2. They're going to tell us how to handle our money to maximize *asset protection* (attorneys).

3. They're going to tell us how to spend and move our money to *reduce our tax liability* (CPAs and attorneys).

So let's talk about these professionals—what they really know, what they're telling you to do, and why they may be your biggest liability.

CHAPTER 8

YOUR FINANCIAL PLANNER

"Many financial advisors recommend that you diversify for your own protection. What they fail to tell you is that it is also for their protection. Since most financial advisors cannot tell you exactly which stock or mutual fund is a great investment, they tell you to buy a bunch of them."

—ROBERT KIYOSAKI

HOW MUCH DO YOU KNOW ABOUT your financial planner/advisor?[1] If you have a 401(k) or other qualified plan, chances are, you have at least interacted with your financial planner to some degree. At the beginning of the process you would have had to express your risk aversion and financial goals in selecting a mutual fund. Other than the initial meeting (or virtual meeting) to set up your fund, the periodic email spam you get from the brokerage firm, and the tax statement you get at the beginning of every year, you probably don't have much interaction with your financial planner at all.

Do you know what a financial planner actually does?

The United States Bureau of Labor and Statistics describes "personal financial advisors" as people who "provide advice to help individuals manage their finances and plan for their financial future."[2] They are supposed to help you invest your money in a way that you can maximize growth based on your financial goals. Do you mind not having access to your money until retirement? They have the plan for you. Do you need a steady stream of income? Different

---

1. For the purposes of this chapter, we will assume that financial planners and financial advisors are the same.
2. "Occupational Outlook Handbook: Personal Financial Advisors," U.S. Bureau of Labor Statistics, April 10, 2020, accessed April 24, 2020, https://www.bls.gov/ooh/business-and-financial/personal-financial-advisors.htm.

plan. Are you good to invest for the long-term, but you still need at least some of the money to be liquid? They've got a plan.

Although that's exactly what financial planners say they do—go search any advisor's profile online to find a repository of financial language flowery enough to make you slightly nauseated—let's distinguish what they say they do from what they actually do. If you have personal experiences you can draw on, please do so to see how much of this rings true for you (and what conclusions you can draw from it).

First, let's look at what it takes to become a financial planner—education, licensing, etc.

FINANCIAL PLANNER EDUCATION REQUIREMENTS

The Bureau of Labor and Statistics website says a financial planner typically needs a bachelor's degree.[3] But is that true? To be licensed as an investment advisor representative, which is the Series 65 license a financial planner needs, you do not need a degree. You just need to pay the $175 fee and get at least a 72 percent on the three-hour, 130-question test.[4] That should alarm you. Your financial planner, to get licensed, had to score at least a C-.

Your financial planner, to get licensed, had to score at least a C-.

3. *Id.*
4. Kaplan Financial Education, "How to Get Your Series 65 License," Kaplan.com, March 18, 2020, last accessed July 8, 2020, https://www.kaplanfinancial.com/resources/career-advancement/how-to-get-your-series-65-license. To sell securities, you must pass the Securities Industry Essentials and Series 7 exams. Neither have any educational prerequisites. FINRA, "Securities Industry Essentials (SIE) Exam," last accessed July 8, 2020, https://www.finra.org/registration-exams-ce/qualification-exams/securities-industry-essentials-exam.

It is no surprise then, that many financial advisory firms do not require a bachelor's degree. Fidelity, Ameriprise Financial, and Edward Jones are among the three biggest financial investment firms, and none of them require a college degree.

Fidelity says, "A college degree is encouraged yet not required."[5] Ameriprise Financial asks for a "high school diploma or equivalent."[6] Edward Jones "prefers" a college degree but does not require one.[7] None of them requires any specialized certificates, courses, or degrees relating to any of these money skills we've been talking about.

We've already reviewed how much we (do not) teach our students about investing and finance in high school. But the dearth of money skills is exactly what qualifies you for a job at an investment firm.

Then, once you've put in your time and learned what you need to pass the licensing exam, you can join the approximately 220,000 financial planners in the country making a median income of $88,890 annually.[8] The bad news is that your investments are what are paying their wages. The good news? At least they aren't making very much money.

The most alarming aspect of the financial planning industry is not the educational prerequisites. It is the advice they are giving people.

---

5. "Fidelity Careers," last accessed April 24, 2020, https://jobs.fidelity.com/ShowJob/Id/909395/Financial-Representative,-Farmington-Hills,-MI/.
6. "Financial Advisor in Training Job," Ameriprise Financial, Lensa.com, last accessed July 8, 2020. https://lensa.com/financial-advisor-in-training-jobs/las-vegas/jd/3ec6e143e9dd586009559dc4c6b1378a.
7. "The Edward Jones Financial Advisor Opportunity," Edwardjones.com, last accessed April 24, 2020, https://careers.edwardjones.com/explore-opportunities/new-financial-advisors/about/job-description.html.
8. "Occupational Outlook Handbook: Personal Financial Advisors," U.S. Bureau of Labor Statistics, April 10, 2020, accessed July 8, 2020, https://www.bls.gov/ooh/business-and-financial/personal-financial-advisors.htm.

YOUR FINANCIAL PLANNER'S ADVICE

The options for investing your money are almost infinite. Besides stocks, bonds, and mutual funds, you could put your money in real estate (fixes and flips, wholesaling, or short- or long-term rentals), certificates of deposit, gold or silver, a business start-up (either your own or someone else's), a franchise, a high-yield savings account, etc.

But the investment options your financial planner has for you are not just finite but very limited.

I remember when I was fifteen years old. My best friend, Jamie Askar, was about six weeks older than me, and he had just turned sixteen. He got his driver's license. For those six weeks before I was licensed to drive, we drove around everywhere in his dad's gray 1980-something model Toyota Tercel hatchback. It was an ugly little thing, even then. We called it the "Turtle."

Because we were teenage boys with brand-new freedoms, we often did stupid things we thought were hilarious.

On one occasion, we went to one of our favorite restaurants—Del Taco. We were in the drive-through line, and Jamie, who was driving, was talking to the Del Taco employee over the intercom.

"Yeah, I'll have two Big Macs, please. Two large fries, and two cups of water."

"We don't have Big Macs. Would you like the Double Del cheeseburger?"

"No. I'm really in the mood for a Big Mac. Just give me the Big Macs."

"This isn't McDonald's. We don't have Big Macs."

"You don't? Well, what do you have?"

"We have the Double Del, which is a double-stack cheeseburger with lettuce, tomatoes, onions, and burger sauce."

"Is that something I could get without onions?"

"Yes."

"And could I get them without tomatoes?"

"Yes, of course."

"Okay. I'll just have the fries and water."

I can see now that this isn't hilarious; it's not even really funny. Nevertheless, it illustrates a good point. When you go to Del Taco, you can order a Double Del, but you can't order a Big Mac. You can't get a Whopper at McDonald's or a Jr. Bacon Cheeseburger at Subway.

When you go to any restaurant, your choices are not unlimited. You can buy what they sell and nothing more.

It's the same when you seek the professional advice of a financial advisor. The financial advisor's answer to your question "What is the best place to invest my money?" is never going to have an answer beyond the products that the brokerage firm offers.

> **The financial advisor's answer to your question "What is the best place to invest my money?" is never going to have an answer beyond the products that the brokerage firm offers.**

Fidelity offers more than 500 mutual funds.[9] Ameriprise will "help you build a portfolio that's right for you, selecting from more than 2,200 funds from nearly 160 fund companies."[10] Edward Jones doesn't quantify the mutual funds available to their clients but boasts having "more than $400 billion in mutual fund assets under care."[11]

---

9. "Fidelity by the Numbers: Corporate Statistics," Fidelity.com, last accessed April 27, 2020, https://www.fidelity.com/about-fidelity/fidelity-by-numbers/corporate-statistics.
10. "Mutual Funds," Ameriprise.com, last accessed April 27, 2020, https://www.ameriprise.com/products-services/investments/mutual-funds/.
11. "What Is a Mutual Fund," Edwardjones.com, last accessed April 27, 2020, https://www.edwardjones.com/investments-services/stocks-bonds-mutual-funds/mutual-funds/overview.html.

Don't make the mistake of thinking that your financial planner is actually telling you the best thing to do with your money any more than the guy at Del Taco is going to tell you where to buy the best burger in town.[12] The financial planner is there to help you choose *which of their funds* you should put your money in, not which of all investment options is best for you. Your financial planner will never recommend real estate. The recommendation is always going to be this fund or that fund.

That presents another issue altogether: Are they even giving you the best advice among the many options available? Every fund carries with it an inherent conflict of interest. Because commissions are paid out of the money you have invested in the market, the higher the commissions to the financial planner, the more potential for growth is lost.

So when a financial planner makes recommendations to you, is it because it is best for you or because it pays the best commission? That is an inherent conflict of interest that most financial planners don't have to disclose.

FIDUCIARY V. SUITABILITY STANDARD

This tug-of-war, where what is better for you is worse for the financial planner and vice versa, is a known conflict of interest. It's one that has caused enough harm that the Department of Labor is trying to do something about it.

Unless your financial planner is charging you flat fees for the services, chances are, their recommendations are governed by the suitability standard.

The suitability standard says that a financial planner should make recommendations based on the client's risk-tolerance and objectives. This is a pretty low bar and gives the financial planner latitude to make a wide range of

---

12. This probably goes without saying, but the best burger in town is not going to be found anywhere that has "taco" in its name.

recommendations. (After all, even the high-commission products are designed to grow.)

In 2016, the Department of Labor issued a rule that would make financial advisors subject to the much higher fiduciary standard. This means they could only make recommendations for their clients that were in their clients' best interests—and disclose conflicts of interest, including the exact fees charged to the client.[13]

The financial planning industry, which apparently did not like being subjected to a standard that put their clients' needs first, did not sit still. Its lobby became involved in multiple lawsuits across the country that challenged the validity of this new rule. Courts were largely ruling in favor of the rule. The United States District Court for the District of Kansas upheld the rule.[14] The Tenth Circuit Court of Appeals affirmed the decision on appeal.[15]

The United States District Court for the Northern District of Texas upheld the new rule.[16] But then in March 2018, on appeal to the Fifth Circuit Court of Appeals, the financial planning industry finally won. (They only needed to win in one court.) The rule was thrown out.[17]

The issue is far from dead. For now, though, most financial planners are not held to the higher fiduciary standard when making recommendations for investments.[18]

But all of this leaves open a broader question—why would financial planners oppose adhering to a higher standard unless what they are doing now does not meet the higher standard?

---

13. "Conflict of Interest Final Rule," Dol.gov, last accessed July 8, 2020, https://www.dol.gov/agencies/ebsa/laws-and-regulations/rules-and-regulations/completed-rulemaking/1210-AB32-2.
14. *Mkt. Synergy Grp., Inc. v. United States Dep't of Labor*, No. 16-CV-4083-DDC-KGS, 2017 WL 661592, at *1 (D. Kan. Feb. 17, 2017), aff'd, 885 F.3d 676 (10th Cir. 2018).
15. *Mkt. Synergy Grp., Inc. v. United States Dep't of Labor*, 885 F.3d 676 (10th Cir. 2018).
16. *Chamber of Commerce of the United States of Am. v. Hugler*, 231 F. Supp. 3d 152 (N.D. Tex. 2017).
17. *Chamber of Commerce of United States of Am. v. United States Dep't. of Labor*, 885 F.3d 360 (5th Cir. 2018).
18. Some states have taken initiative and applied the rule to advisors within the state.

To answer that, just think about your own experience with your financial planner. If their job is to help maximize your portfolio growth, then in addition to helping you decide *what* products to purchase, shouldn't they also be advising you as to *when* to buy and sell?

You've probably heard that you should "buy low and sell high." Anyone who looks and understands the graph of growth and losses in the stock market over time can see that is true. If you knew exactly what the stock market was going to do, you would know precisely when to buy and when to sell, and you would never need to work another day of your life. You could start with a dollar and retire a billionaire.

Your financial planner will be the first to tell you that through the broker they work for, they are tapped into some of the best financial experts who have beaten the S&P or Dow Jones for gains for several years in a row. That's part of their sales pitch.

The stock market, as measured by the Dow Jones Industrial Average, hit an all-time high twenty-two times in 2019.[19] It hit several new records in 2020, and reached its all-time high of 29,551.42 on February 12, 2020.[20]

Did your financial planner call you at any point in 2019 or 2020, when the stock market had never been higher, to tell you that it was time to sell? Did your financial planner, who understands and has been taught the "buy-low-sell-high" principle, ever tell you to sell high? Did your financial planner, who only makes money off of your account when your money is in the market, ever call you at all?

No. That call never happened. It never happened because your financial planner is more interested in making money than making you money. It never happened because financial planners have abandoned the "buy-low-sell-high" rule of thumb for a new mantra: "Buy always and sell never."

---

19. Staff Writer, "What is the Dow Jones Industrial Average (DIJA) All-Time High?" Investopedia.com, April 12, 2020, last accessed April 30, 2020, https://www.investopedia.com/ask/answers/100214/what-dow-jones-industrial-average-djia-alltime-high.asp.
20. *Id.*

Financial planners have abandoned the "buy-low-sell-high" rule of thumb for a new mantra: "Buy always and sell never."

Indeed, when the stock market was at its highest, financial planners were not telling people to hold off to buy until there was a drop. They were telling people to take advantage of the upward climb.

I had a modest 401(k) resulting from some employer contributions early in my career.[21] In 2019, after seeing over ten years of good growth, I decided it was time to sell. I called my financial planner and told him to take my money out of the market.

My financial planner resisted, explaining to me that the market showed no signs of slowing down, that I would be giving up some amazing gains, and that it wasn't the right time to sell.

Well, if selling when the market is at record highs is not the right time to sell, then when is the right time?

I had to be forceful in my request. The financial planner reluctantly pulled my money out of the market.

I don't have a financial planner anymore.

And yes, another nine months of market growth went by after my money was no longer in the market. But I didn't let myself get psyched out. I knew that historically, the stock market corrects on average every 9.875 years. And it did. Due to the government's response to COVID-19, the stock market took its biggest dip in over a decade.

Some of my clients have not had the same "positive" experience I had. We have clients tell us all the time that when they ask to have their money taken out of the market, their financial planners won't let them. They make up all sort of reasons it can't be done.

---

21. And in case you were wondering, no, I never contributed a dime to this government-sponsored tax plan.

In the last two months, we had a client fighting with his financial planner to do just that. He was taken through the ringer. It took about six weeks for the client to finally get the money removed. He lost $83,000 in those weeks that the financial planner was dragging his feet. The financial planner probably made a couple of hundred bucks by having the client's money under management for those extra six weeks because the financial planner is making money even when you're losing money.

I don't know the end of that story yet, but I understand the client is going to seek to hold the financial planner accountable for that loss.[22]

If you were to challenge these financial planners for their poor advice during the market upswing, they will tell you that no one could have imagined or predicted that the world's governments would shut down the world's economy in response to a viral outbreak, causing a stock market decline. For sure, that's the kind of thing that used to be relegated to sci-fi and zombie films, not reality.

But we've never been able to predict the cause. Steep stock market declines have been attributed in the past to, among many others, overproduction of agricultural produce,[23] the JFK assassination,[24] overspeculation of the value of internet companies,[25] and the housing bubble burst.[26] But anyone who can see

22. I was involved in a similar dispute on behalf of a client. We went through FINRA (Financial Industry Regulatory Authority) and had to prove that the financial advisor was putting his own interests ahead of the client's instead of putting him in an investment "suitable" to his stated goals, which resulted in higher commissions to the financial planner and significant losses to the client. The brokerage firm, which had created tempting incentives for the financial planner to sell the particular product, settled and paid my client.

23. Dan Bryan, "The Great (Farm) Depression of the 1920s," americanhistoryusa.com, March 6, 2012, last accessed April 30, 2020, https://www.americanhistoryusa.com/great-farm-depression-1920s/.

24. Adam Shell, "Stock Impact of JFK Murder Steep but Short," USA Today, November 21, 2013, last accessed July 8, 2020, https://www.usatoday.com/story/money/markets/2013/11/21/stock-market-reaction-to-jfk-assassination/3662171/.

25. Annie Lowrey, "More Money Than Anyone Imagined," The Atlantic, July 26, 2019, last accessed July 8, 2020, https://www.theatlantic.com/ideas/archive/2019/07/whatever-happened-tech-bubble/594856/.

26. Vikas Bajaj, "Top Lender Sees Mortgage Woes for 'Good' Risks," New York Times, July 25, 2007, last accessed April 30, 2020, https://www.nytimes.com/2007/07/25/business/25lend.html.

patterns in a graph could have predicted the correction. Not why. Not exactly when. But we knew it would come.

And now that the stock market has dropped, do you know what your financial planner is saying? They're echoing the same familiar refrain: "It's time to put your money in the market"—the same thing they always say.

Even a broken clock is right twice a day.

CHAPTER 9

YOUR ATTORNEY

"A lawyer is a person who writes a 10,000-word document and calls it a 'brief.'"

—Franz Kafka

WHEREAS YOUR FINANCIAL PLANNER'S ROLE is to help grow your money, usually the attorney's role is more to protect it—keep others from getting to it. Unlike your financial planner, though, your attorney is required to at least have an education. In most states, to even qualify to sit for the bar, an individual must first get through high school, earn a four-year college degree, and attend law school, which is another three years. Having successfully completed this education, they receive their juris doctor degree.

No, the problem with your attorneys is not their lack of education. And their advice is probably sound. It just isn't necessarily solving the right problems.

When it comes to these money skills, you are generally going to seek advice from one of three different kinds of attorneys: a corporate transactional attorney, an estate planning attorney, or a tax attorney. They all focus their practices on different aspects that could be a benefit to you, but rarely do they understand all three in a way that they can provide you with a comprehensive plan.

THE CORPORATE TRANSACTIONAL ATTORNEY

When you picture an attorney, you're probably picturing a litigator or trial attorney—the ones who go to court to represent their client, either prosecuting the case or defending it, making arguments before the judge and the jury. Those are the attorneys most commonly depicted in television and movies.

93

But in many ways, trial attorneys are the antithesis of a corporate transactional attorney. A corporate transactional attorney is one who spends their time drafting documents. Contracts. Operating agreements. Partnership agreements. Bylaws. They're setting up entities for you: limited liability companies, partnerships, and corporations.

Do you remember those "I'm a Mac. I'm a PC" commercials that aired in the first decade of the 2000s as part of Apple's "Get a Mac" campaign? The Mac character, played by Justin Long, was the cool, charismatic character. The PC, played by John Hodgman, was always in a suit, more uptight, and although likeable, was kind of out of touch.

If a litigator is a Mac, then the transactional attorney is the PC. The transactional attorney spends their days researching and writing and will never be found addressing a jury, a judge, or even stepping foot inside the courtroom.

That's not to say that there is anything wrong with the transactional attorney. However, who would you trust to know best how to protect you—the one who has extensively researched the best way to protect you, or the one who has actually been in the courtroom and has stripped entities clean of their protections, pierced corporate veils, and knows exactly where these entities are vulnerable?

Unfortunately, the litigators aren't hiring themselves out to help you set up your businesses. They're too busy in court. That leaves the transactional attorney.

If you were to hire a corporate transactional attorney to set up a business entity for you, you would get a business entity. If you ask the attorney what kind of entity is best for your business, that attorney will explain to you the different attributes of each entity type and how each protects you.

Again, the problem is not so much the attorney or the advice, but that you're asking the wrong questions. If you ask the attorney, "How can I make sure my personal assets are protected from liabilities and obligations of the business?" the attorney will be able to explain to you about corporate protections, corporate formalities, and the corporate veil. They'll probably be right on the money, even if their entire experience with the protections is theoretical.

But if you ask the attorney, "How should I structure my business life and personal life to maximize creditor protection from *all* liabilities and obligations while minimizing my tax burden irrespective of my income?" that corporate transactional attorney, if honest, will most likely tell you that much of what you're asking is beyond the scope of what they can do.

What good does it do you to protect yourself from corporate liabilities if, in the process, you are increasing your tax rate or opening yourself up to other liabilities?

Having the Wrong Business Setup Can Create More Liability

Almost exactly one year before the writing of this book, I was in trial. I represented an attorney in Ohio against an attorney in Las Vegas. The Las Vegas attorney had hired the Ohio attorney, chose not to pay the Ohio attorney for his services, and then the Ohio attorney got a judgment against the Las Vegas attorney.[1]

Because the Las Vegas attorney had assets in Nevada, which is where I practice, the Ohio attorney hired me to help execute the judgment by collecting the Nevada assets.

The judgment was against the Las Vegas attorney personally and did not implicate any of his businesses. Further, the Las Vegas attorney fancied himself an expert on money and structures. However, contrary to what an expert or even a smart attorney would do, the Las Vegas attorney transferred many of his personal assets to his family limited partnership, his trust, and his corporation.

In response, we filed a lawsuit against the Las Vegas attorney attempting to do what is called a "reverse corporate veil piercing," where the law holds an entity liable for an individual's debts.

---

1. Yes, that sounds like the beginning of a lawyer joke. Unfortunately, it was just the beginning of a tragedy.

That is what last year's trial was about.

Ultimately, we were successful. When we started, we only had a judgment against the Las Vegas attorney individually. Afterward, that same judgment could be levied against any of the Las Vegas attorney's personal assets, his family limited partnership's assets, his trust's assets, and his corporation's assets.

The moral of that story is that it doesn't matter which entities you have or how many. What matters is that they are set up correctly and for the right reasons. If you set them up wrong, you can actually *increase* liability rather than protect against it.

> **It doesn't matter which entities you have or how many. What matters is that they are set up correctly and for the right reasons. If you set them up wrong, you can actually increase liability rather than protect against it.**

Sometimes an Entity, Even If Set up Right, Doesn't Protect You at All

One purpose of creating a business entity—partnership, limited liability company, or corporation—is to add a separate layer of protection between you and the people that entity interacts with.

If you do business as a sole proprietor, which means you haven't set up a business at all and are just in business as yourself, then any liabilities your business incurs are liabilities you have to pay out of your individual assets. There is no separate entity or ownership, so all liabilities and assets of either of you are liabilities and assets of both of you.

If you create an entity, though, you are actually creating a new "person" under the law, something that can have its own liabilities and its own assets. Then, if that entity becomes liable in some way—maybe it breaches a lease, or someone gets hurt on its premises—the liability ends with the company. You don't have to come out of pocket personally.

In many cases, that's exactly how it works. If you slip and fall at a McDonald's, Burger King is not at all responsible, or liable, for your loss. McDonald's is. To think that you could hold one accountable for the actions of the other sounds absurd. But those protections don't just extend to two unrelated entities. It also extends to you, if done correctly.

For example, Ray Kroc was the founder of the McDonald's corporation. He is no longer alive, but if he were, and someone were to slip and fall at a McDonald's because an employee left vanilla ice cream on the floor, only McDonald's would be responsible, not Ray Kroc personally. Because just like Burger King is not McDonald's, neither is Ray Kroc McDonald's.

That is exactly why people set up entities—to make sure their assets are not in danger from their business's liabilities.

But it doesn't always work that way. I do a lot of business with physicians and dentists who own their own practices. Every single one of them had the foresight to set up a business entity—usually either a limited liability company or corporation. And every single one thinks that protects them. But it really doesn't.

Think for a moment—why would setting up a corporation protect someone like Ray Kroc but not a doctor? It's not really a legal question so much as a common sense one.

Remember, one purpose of a business entity like a corporation is to provide protection of *individual* assets against *corporate* liabilities. If you are a small business owner, like a doctor, you do business much differently than McDonald's.

Every single one of you reading this book has undoubtedly eaten at McDonald's, but I would be surprised if any of you have ever met Ray Kroc. You've all been to Wal-Mart but probably never interacted with any member of the Walton family.

In fact, if you were to get injured at McDonald's or Wal-Mart, would it even cross your mind to figure out who succeeded Ray Kroc as owner or to track down bank accounts of the surviving Walton family? Probably not. Even if it did, your attorney would know better, and that demand letter is going to go to a department in McDonald's or Wal-Mart corporate. The owners don't even enter the picture because you never interacted with them, and you don't have any sense that they are individually accountable. The business is.

But that's different for a small business owner. When someone asks you for a referral, do you give them the name of your doctor, or do you give them the name of your doctor's business entity (which may or may not be the same as the name on the sign out front)? When you go to your dentist, you actually interact with your dentist. He or she actually touches you. X-rays you. Drills into you. Which means when something goes wrong, it's your dentist you look to for answers, not their business entity.

Many of my clients are surprised to know that their corporate entity provides them with very little protection. Sure, it might protect them personally from contract damages incurred by their entity, but it's not protecting them from patients. Not even a little bit. That's not because their attorney set up the entity wrong, but because it was never designed to protect them against patients. You wouldn't expect a bulletproof vest to protect you against headshots. If you're worried about shots to the head, you wear a helmet.

Creating a liability shield to keep more of your money is more complicated than just setting up a business entity. As your corporate transactional attorney will admit, if you know to ask, much of these protections go far beyond what they are capable of doing. You need someone who sees the big picture and understands all the moving parts.

THE ESTATE PLANNING ATTORNEY

The estate planning attorney has a different role altogether when it comes to protecting your assets. Much of what an estate planning attorney does relates to what happens with your estate when you pass on. Their goal is to make sure the process is seamless, avoiding probate (the court's involvement with the distribution of assets in your estate after you die), minimizing the estate tax, and having the wishes in your will carried out.

Some of what they do also applies when you are still alive but incapacitated—medical directives and a power of attorney, for example. Both speak for you when you cannot to ensure that your wishes are carried out.

A revocable living trust can perform those functions—express your desires, appoint people to make decisions on your behalf when you cannot, appoint a guardian for your children, and help you avoid probate, to name a few.

But estate planning attorneys also usually offer asset protection strategies, too. These strategies are probably going to involve an irrevocable trust, if you set it up in one of the minority of states that allows it, and a domestic asset protection trust.

Irrevocable Trusts

Often, wealthy people use irrevocable trusts as a way to create a positive legacy. When you hear the term "trust fund baby," that's an irrevocable trust.[2]

If a wealthy person has a lot of money to pass on, accumulated over a lifetime of hard work, savvy investing, and discipline, they don't necessarily want their kids getting it in one lump sum and squandering it. They want that money to be used for good—to enhance, not mar, their legacy. So, upon their death, the irrevocable trust distributes money to those kids—beneficiaries of the irrevocable trust—over time. Perhaps they get a monthly allotment. They can probably apply for bigger sums if they need it to pay school tuition or for medical reasons. The person establishing the trust gets to choose those terms.

---

2. The same thing can be created by a revocable trust, which becomes irrevocable when the grantor dies.

Of course, under these circumstances, the irrevocable trust is more of an estate planning tool than an asset protection tool. It can serve to protect assets, though, if those assets are transferred into the trust during the grantor's lifetime.

An irrevocable trust, like a business entity, is an entity separate in the law. There really is no possibility of liability from a trust, since it does not occupy a physical space and does not interact with people like a business or person does.

The purpose of an irrevocable trust is not to separate its liability from your own, but rather to create a place where you can put your assets where your personal creditors cannot reach them. It does this by splitting and assigning legal and equitable ownership.[3]

There are essentially three parties to a trust. The trustor (you) establishes the trust and determines the terms of the trust.[4] You give up ownership of the assets in the trust and give up control to the trust through the permanent terms you choose and cannot later change.

You appoint a third party, the trustee, and by creating the trust, you transfer legal title of the assets in the trust to the trustee. This grants the trustee control over the assets, but only within the parameters set by the terms of the trust and for the benefit of the beneficiaries. Because the trustee's legal ownership is subject to these limited terms, creditors of the trust cannot take assets from the trustee.

You also designate beneficiaries of the trust. They have no legal ownership and therefore no right to dictate what happens to the assets in the trust. However, they have equitable title, which means the assets in the trust must benefit them even if they have no control over how, when, why, or how much. If a beneficiary has a future right to the money, then creditors can attach that. However, to prevent this, irrevocable trusts will include a spendthrift provision, which prevents the beneficiaries from selling or

3. Eric Boughman, "Using Self-Settled Trusts," forbes.com, February 9, 2017, last accessed July 8, 2020, https://www.forbes.com/sites/forbeslegalcouncil/2017/02/09/practical-considerations-for-using-self-settled-trusts.
4. Also called "the grantor" or "the settlor."

incumbering future trust assets. So creditors cannot attach to the beneficiaries' equitable ownership, either.

If set up correctly, a creditor cannot get at the assets of an irrevocable trust through the trustor (because the trustor has no ownership rights anymore), the trustee (because the trustee's ownership is legal only with no rights of possession or use, just distribution), nor the beneficiary (whose future interests cannot be attached because of the spendthrift provision).

This only works because when you put assets in an irrevocable trust, you give up both ownership and control. Those assets are not yours anymore. Now they belong to the trust and are controlled by the trustee, subject to the terms of the trust, which as mentioned earlier, you dictated and cannot change after the trust is created (that's what the term "irrevocable" means in the title).

An irrevocable trust set up like this does a really good job protecting your assets. But it comes at a cost—those assets are not yours anymore. If you change your mind and want them back, that's not going to happen.

To solve that problem, some states (nineteen at the time of this writing) recognize a certain type of irrevocable trust called an "asset protection trust," also called a "self-settled trust."

In this trust, the trustor and the beneficiaries are the same person (you). A third party still must serve as trustee, and once the terms of the trust are set, you cannot change them (it is still irrevocable). However, you can put your money in the trust where it will be protected as long as it remains there. The trustee can distribute money back to you per the terms of the trust.

If done correctly, your assets can be protected without giving up significant rights related to the assets. If you reside in one of the nineteen states that offers them,[5] your estate planning attorney can undoubtedly create one for you.

---

5. The nineteen states that allow asset protection trusts as of 2020 are Alaska, Connecticut, Delaware, Hawaii, Indiana, Michigan, Mississippi, Missouri, Nevada, New Hampshire, Ohio, Oklahoma, Rhode Island, South Dakota, Tennessee, Utah, Virginia, West Virginia, and Wyoming.

Even if you do not live in one of these nineteen states, you can set one up, but there are significant potential pitfalls if you don't do it right.

Conflicts of Laws and the Asset Protection Trust

Because only a minority of states recognize the asset protection trust, care must be used in setting up these types of trusts for residents of those states that don't recognize them. In fact, although more and more states are adopting the asset protection trust, some states are strongly opposed to any instrument that allows such a benefit to a debtor at the expense of a creditor.[6]

Problems can potentially arise if you live in one of these latter thirty-one states but set up an asset protection trust in one of the nineteen that allows it.

One such problem arose in Washington. Washington has a strong public policy against asset protection trusts.[7] However, one Donald G. Huber, a real estate developer, began running into significant financial troubles related to the market crash in 2008.[8] His creditors started pressuring him to pay. In an effort to protect his assets, he established an asset protection trust in Alaska, one of the states that allows such trusts.[9] He then transferred several of his assets into his trust, and sometime after that, filed for bankruptcy.

One of his creditors sought to invalidate the trust and the transfers. The bankruptcy court had to determine whether Alaska law applied to the trust, in

---

6. *E.g., Matter of Shurley*, 115 F.3d 333, 338 (5th Cir. 1997) ("Public policy does not countenance devices by which one frees his own property from liability for his debts or restricts his power of alienation of it; and it is accordingly universally recognized that one cannot settle upon himself a spendthrift or other protective trust, or purchase such a trust from another, which will be effective to protect either the income or the corpus against the claims of his creditors, or to free it from his own power of alienation. The rule applies in respect of both present and future creditors and irrespective of any fraudulent intent in the settlement or purchase of a trust.") *See also In re Zukerkorn*, 484 B.R. 182, 193 (B.A.P. 9th Cir. 2012) *and In re Lewiston*, 532 B.R. 36, 39 (Bankr. E.D. Mich. 2015).
7. Rev. Code Wash. 19.36.020.
8. *In re Huber*, 493 B.R. 798, 806 (Bankr. W.D. Wash. 2013).
9. Al. Stat. 34.40.110.

which case the trust would have been valid (though the transfer may not have been), or Washington law, in which the trust would not have been valid.

Part of Huber's problem was that he did not create the trust ahead of time and only did so once he had creditors. Such a transfer is known as a fraudulent transfer, and an asset protection trust typically will not protect against a fraudulent transfer. In fact, even if Washington had recognized the Alaska trust, his transfer would not have been valid as it was done *after* the debt was incurred, in hopes of preventing known creditors from reaching the assets. It would have been considered an attempt to defraud his creditors.[10]

But even without the fraudulent transfer, his use of an Alaska trust was invalidated because there was not a sufficient nexus, or connection, to Alaska: the debtor resided in Washington, almost all of the property placed in the trust was located in Washington, the trust beneficiaries were Washington residents, and the attorney who prepared the trust documents and transferred assets into the trust was in Washington.[11] Washington, therefore, applied its own state law, and the trust itself was rendered void, obviating the asset protection.

This case demonstrates the importance of setting up an asset protection trust correctly. It also demonstrates the shortsightedness of the estate planning attorney. This trust had a single, focused purpose: to keep the trustor's assets out of the hands of the creditors. The idea that that is possible in some states is repugnant in others. From the very beginning, the trust was doomed to fail.

Because the estate planning attorney had tunnel vision, the product he created, which had one job—protect assets—failed at its job.

Instead, had the asset protection trust not just been designed to keep money out of creditors' hands but been a part of a larger structure—each part with a legitimate purpose and role that pre-existed any of the trustor's debts—it would have had a much better chance of being seen as legitimate rather than a transparent attempt to defraud a Washington creditor.

10. *Huber,* 493 B.R. at 813–14.
11. *Id.* at 808–09.

For example, if the asset protection trust was a limited partner in a partnership with a legitimate business purpose, it would have been fulfilling a necessary and productive role, which would make Washington judges less suspicious of it from the beginning. Further, it would have created additional ties to Alaska, which was the ultimate issue that decided the trust's validity.

This approach is problematic for the estate planning attorney, though, because the estate planning attorney does not set up the entities. The estate planning attorney doesn't have the knowledge or resources of the corporate transactional attorney nor the practical experience of the litigator. To take advantage of the real benefit of an asset protection trust, you would need both an estate planning attorney and an attorney who understands entities. Or someone who understands both.

THE TAX ATTORNEY

Tax attorneys come in many different forms. A tax attorney will typically specialize in one or more specific areas of tax law, including audits and appeals, compliance, corporate tax, employee benefits, estate and generation-skipping taxes, international tax law, litigation, mergers and acquisitions, real estate, state and local tax, or tax-exempt organizations.[12]

In addition to a juris doctor degree, many tax attorneys also have a master of laws degree in taxes, or LL.M., which requires an additional year of study.

Tax attorneys are the ones speaking up when new tax laws go into effect, announcing what the laws mean and what the big implications are.

The issue with your attorneys is that they're addressing only limited-scope issues without regard to what effect that is going to have on the rest of your plans. You don't just want a plan that reduces your taxes. You want your assets

---

12. Jessica Tomer, "Want to Be a Happy Lawyer? Study Tax Law," New England Law Boston, last accessed April 28, 2020, https://www.nesl.edu/news/detail/want-to-be-a-happy-lawyer-study-tax-law-(9-reasons-why-you-should).

and investments to be safe too. That's not something that is necessarily on their radar, and even if you bring it to their attention, it likely won't be something they know how to address.

If you want to hire a tax lawyer, usually you're going to have to retain a large firm with a tax division. That means tax lawyers are very expensive, so unless you're in several-digit trouble with the IRS, very wealthy, or a large corporation, you probably aren't going to be hiring a tax attorney any time soon.

CHAPTER 10

YOUR CERTIFIED PUBLIC ACCOUNTANT

"People always ask me, 'Were you funny as a child?'
Well, no, I was an accountant."
—ELLEN DEGENERES

WHEN IT COMES TIME TO FILE OUR TAXES every year, if we're going to turn to anyone for help, it is likely going to be a CPA. After all, that's a big part of what CPAs do—file taxes.

You may have never thought of it this way, but that tax return you have to file every year may be the single most important financial transaction you are a part of that year. Depending on the outcome, it could be the biggest check you receive—a critical part of your financial planning for the home remodel, debt repayment, or nest-egg contribution.[1]

If you are surprised with a huge tax hit, that could be devastating and set you back for years.

If your returns are not filed correctly, things could be even worse. You could overpay in taxes and not know it. You could underpay and then later be subjected to fines, penalties, and back taxes. You could also be subjected to criminal liability.

You may already realize this. Maybe that's why you hire a CPA—to make sure your taxes are done right. But how confident are you that your CPA is doing things right?

---

1. If the tax refund check is your biggest check, and you rely on it as part of your budget planning, then you're not planning right.

MOST PROFESSIONALLY PREPARED TAX RETURNS ARE WRONG

In the last several years, many different organizations have conducted "mystery shopper" audits of tax preparer work. This included major chains, CPAs, and other independent preparers. Mystery shoppers would present one of two tax scenarios to a paid tax preparer, pay the tax preparer to prepare the tax form, and then take the tax form back to be analyzed for accuracy.

In one of the more recent and detailed studies published by the National Consumer Law Center, the two tax scenarios were not complex.[2]

Scenario one was a single parent with one child earning $22,000 annually as an employee and $800 annually as an independent contractor (1099) for a side business selling trinkets. Scenario two was a graduate student who earned $9,180 from a paid internship as a 1099 with $1,520 in investment income from mutual fund distributions. The student also had a student loan and a small grant to pay for tuition.

The two scenarios were carried out a total of twenty-nine times in combination by different tax preparers, and twenty-seven of the twenty-nine (93.1 percent) were prepared incorrectly.[3] These results are not anomalous. The same study reported results of similar past studies done between 2006 and 2014, and they showed that between 25 percent and 90 percent of returns were prepared incorrectly. Taking those studies together, on average, 69.1 percent of all returns tested were prepared incorrectly.[4]

> ***On average, 69.1 percent of all returns tested were prepared incorrectly.***

---

2. Chi Chi Wu, "Prepared in Error: Mystery Shoppers in Florida and North Carolina Uncover Serious Tax Preparer Problems," National Consumer Law Center, April 2015, last accessed May 1, 2020, https://www.nclc.org/images/pdf/pr-reports/report-prepared-in-error.pdf.
3. *Id.* at iii.
4. *Id.* at 2.

Tax preparation fees for scenario one ranged from $37 to $427 (with an average of $148.67), and the taxes ranged from $222 owed to a $4,379 refund (average of $2,277.33 in refunds).

Tax preparation fees for scenario two ranged from $50 to $341 (with an average of $145.82), and the taxes ranged from $1,180 owed to a $1,000 refund (with an average of $221.93 owed).

There was a positive correlation between the size of the refund and the cost to prepare the return. In scenario two, where in most cases there was no refund, the correlation was slight.[5] Where there was money to be refunded (scenario one), the relationship between the cost of preparation and size of return was over twice what it was in scenario two.[6]

The fact that there is any correlation at all should be alarming as the IRS prohibits tax preparers from basing their fees on the amount refunded.[7] Presumably, this is to prevent CPAs and other tax preparers from artificially (and dishonestly) increasing your tax return amount to justify charging more money.

These problems are due, at least in part, to two facts: (1) forty-six states do not regulate tax preparers and have no minimum educational or competency standards for tax preparers,[8] and (2) when your CPA makes a mistake on your taxes that results in your underpaying taxes (or getting a bigger refund than you should), you are the one responsible for paying the difference, not the CPA.[9] Although the CPA may be penalized between $50 and $500 for each error,

5. The R^2 value was 0.1454 on a scale where 1 is a perfect negative correlation, 0 means no correlation, and 1 is a perfect positive correlation. If a tax preparer charged a percentage of every dollar refunded, for example, there would be a perfect positive correlation, and the R^2 value would be 1.
6. The R^2 value in scenario 1 was 0.3929.
7. "Treasury Department Circular No. 230, Regulations Governing Practice Before the Internal Revenue Service: Title 31 Code of Federal Regulations, Subtitle A, Part 10, § 10.27(b)–(c)" Internal Revenue Service, June 12, 2014, last accessed May 1, 2020, https://www.irs.gov/pub/irs-pdf/pcir230.pdf.
8. "Prepared in Error" at 1.
9. RJS Law, "Can Tax Preparers Be Liable for Tax Mistakes?" Irssolution.com, last accessed May 1, 2020, https://irssolution.com/blog/tax-preparers-liable-tax-mistakes.

you're the one left with the tax bill, and depending on the circumstances, you could be fined too.[10]

YOUR CPA HAS A LOWER INCOME THAN YOU

Accountants and auditors, including CPAs, have an annual median income of $71,550 per year.[11] That's barely higher than the $63,179 median income for all U.S. households.[12]

And it's no wonder. The National Society of Accountants surveyed a number of tax accounting firms nationally and calculated the average fee for a Form 1040 with itemized deductions and a state filing was $294.[13] For a nonitemized return, the average fee is only $188.[14] When doing hourly work, the average fee is $158 per hour for federal and state returns.[15]

---

10. *See* 26 U.S.C. 6695.

11. "Occupational Outlook Handbook: Accountants and Auditors," U.S. Bureau of Labor Statistics, last modified April 10, 2020, last accessed May 1, 2020, https://www.bls.gov/ooh/business-and-financial/accountants-and-auditors.htm.

12. "Income and Poverty in the United States: 2018, Table A-2," U.S. Census Bureau, September 2019, last accessed May 1, 2020, https://www.census.gov/data/tables/2019/demo/income-poverty/p60-266.html.

13. "2018–19 Income & Fees of Accountants and Tax Preparers in Public Practice Survey Report," National Society of Accountants Main Street Practitioner, last accessed May 1, 2020, https://mainstreetpractitioner.org/feature/nsas-2018-2019-income-and-fee-survey-is-here.

14. *Id.*

15. *Id.* Doing a little math raises some other questions. If the median income for an accountant is $71,550, but the average hourly rate is $158, that equates to 452 hours of work per year, which is about 8.70 hours per week. If accountants were charging $158 hourly for 40 hours per week, 52 weeks per year, their income would be $328,640. Granted, it's not fair to equate take-away pay with gross hourly rate, since business owners have several expenses before they take any money home. However if someone is bringing in $318,640 but only taking home $77,550, there is something seriously wrong with their business model or their math.

That means a CPA starts losing money if they spend more than an hour and 11 minutes on your nonitemized return.[16]

How much thought and effort do you think your CPA is putting into your federal- and state-mandated tax filings? If it is to be worth their time, they've got to get it done in less than seventy-one minutes.

Have you ever sat down with your CPA while they were doing your taxes? Typically, all they're doing is taking information from your receipts and various tax forms: W2, 1099, 1098,[17] 1098-E,[18] etc. and plugging them into software on their computer.

Then they hit the green button, show you the draft, and ask if everything looks good.

It's at that point when you look through it and see that your refund is smaller than you thought (or that you owe more than you thought) that you start asking about deductions.

"What about the receipts I gave you for the construction of my home office?"

"What about the info I gave you showing how I used my vehicle for work use?"

"What about the money I donated to charity?"

As you remind your CPA about the deductions, they enter numbers into a few more boxes, and the output numbers look better.

Once you're satisfied your CPA has included everything you could think of, you sign the forms, and they get submitted.

But then you wonder why you're the one who had to figure out what deductions you might qualify for. And that makes you wonder what else you might have been able to take advantage of that you, untrained in taxes as you are, wouldn't have known to consider or research.

---

16. An hour and 11 minutes is how long a CPA would have to work earning $158 per hour to earn $188. If they have to spend longer than that on a nonitemized return, it becomes a better use of their time to do some of their hourly work.

17. That's the mortgage interest statement.

18. That's the student loan interest statement.

Part of that is because CPAs rely heavily on software. Indeed, in an annual survey the Journal of Accountancy conducts, rather than asking *whether* CPAs use tax software, it's assumed that all CPAs use one software or another to prepare taxes.[19] Preparing taxes has become more about accurate data entry than creativity and proactive tax planning.

Because your CPA's tax knowledge is mostly centered around deductions, if you do rely on your CPA for tax-planning advice during the tax year, that advice is most likely going to be aimed at increasing your deductions to decrease what you pay in taxes, even if it means you're taking less money home.

> *Because your CPA's tax knowledge is mostly centered around deductions, if you do rely on your CPA for tax-planning advice during the tax year, that advice is most likely going to be aimed at increasing your deductions to decrease what you pay in taxes, even if it means you're taking less money home.*

I have had more than one client who, as part of their tax planning, purchases a new vehicle—usually a truck—every year or two. Under the current rules, the section 179 deduction allows you to deduct, in the year you purchase the vehicle, the percent of the vehicle you use for business (if it is at least 50 percent) up to $25,000 for most vehicles.[20] Other vehicles, like those that can seat at least ten people (large vans) and long-bed pickup trucks (with beds that are at least six feet long) are not subject to the $25,000 limit.[21]

---

19. Paul Bonner, *Journal of Accountancy*, "2019 Tax Software Survey," September 1, 2019, last accessed July 8, 2020, https://www.journalofaccountancy.com/issues/2019/sep/2019-tax-software-survey.html.
20. 26 U.S.C. 179(b)(5).
21. *Id.*

So if you purchase a $50,000 long-bed truck every year, you get a huge tax deduction every year. Let's say you use your truck 75 percent for business and 25 percent for personal use. That means you get a $37,500 tax deduction, meaning your taxable income decreases by $37,500.

That sounds huge! Plus, you have an excuse to buy a new car every year. And you feel smart because that new car you get every year actually saves you money.

But does it?

Let's do the math. If you are purchasing a nice new car every year, you're probably (hopefully) making at least $200,000. Let's assume that's your annual income. At the 2020 tax brackets, that puts you in the 32 percent bracket.[22] With your other deductions, let's say your taxable income is actually around $175,000. When you purchase your $50,000 truck and deduct $37,500, it takes your taxable income down to $137,500. So now you're in the 24 percent tax bracket.

Your tax bill is going to be $26,959.50.[23]

If you hadn't purchased the truck, you would have had to pay taxes at up to a 32 percent rate on $175,000. That's $36,775.50 total. So by purchasing a new vehicle, you save $9,816.00 in taxes! That's awesome, right?

Yes, if you think spending $50,000 to save $9,816 is awesome.[24]

You have effectively purchased a $50,000 truck for only $40,184. That is a killer deal. But only if you actually needed a truck and were going to buy one anyway. Otherwise, you're just spending $40,184 that you don't need to spend.

22. $163,301 to $207,350 for single filers.
23. That's calculated by taking $137,000 and dividing it up into all the tax brackets. The first $9,875 will be taxed at 10%, the next $30,250 will be taxed at 12%, the next $34,400 at 22%, and the last $51,475 at 24%.
24. Of course, if you're the type of person who would rather send $50,000 to a car dealership than send $25,000 to the government, then by all means, continue to waste your money.

Put another way, in scenario one (where you only pay $26,959.50 in taxes), you take home $123,040.50 after paying taxes and purchasing your truck.[25] In scenario two, you take home $163,224.50 after paying taxes and not purchasing your truck.[26]

If you are purchasing a new vehicle for your business, by all means take advantage of those tax savings. But if your CPA is telling you to buy a new vehicle every year or every two years, you have to wonder what kind of math they're using to conclude that stepping on a dollar to save a dime makes sense.[27]

The goal should not be to just pay less in taxes, even if that means you take less home. The goal should be for you to pay less in taxes so you can keep *more* of your money. A CPA focuses on the former. They are not built for, focused on, nor equipped for the latter.

---

25. $200,000 gross earnings less $26,959.50 in taxes and $50,000 for the truck.
26. $200,000 gross earnings less $36,775.50 in taxes.
27. Or cents. See what I did there?

CHAPTER 11

ANALYSIS PARALYSIS

"Lawyers are just like physicians: what one says,
the other contradicts."

– Sholem Aleichem

WHEN YOU ARE PROACTIVE and want to set yourself up to protect your assets, reduce your taxes, get involved in sound investments, etc. (remember those money skills?), you probably aren't sure where to go.

If you were a member of the top 1 percent of income earners, you'd go to a big firm with a tax department, corporate department, estate planning, etc., and you would pay tens of thousands of dollars a year to save hundreds of thousands in taxes. And what you spend is going to be worth every penny.

But if you aren't earning enough to save hundreds of thousands in taxes, those services are not available to you—they're cost prohibitive. Instead, you find yourself wondering what you should be doing to keep more of your money, grow your money, and protect your money. That's why you're relying on the financial planner, the CPA, and maybe attorneys. They're "professionals," after all.[1] Trying to manage your affairs with all these different professionals can be a frustrating, time-consuming, expensive, and confusing ordeal.

For example, let's imagine that you want to start a business. You live in a state with high income tax, say California, where they take back up to 13.3 percent of your income. In a world where starting a business comes with no guarantees, that extra 13.3 percent loss will really slow you down and could make ongoing profitability impossible.

---

1. Although we tend to give added weight to a professional's opinion, the term "professional," in a literal sense, just means that someone gets paid to do it: "professional, adjective: pro-fes-sion-al | \ prə-ˈfesh-nəl: engaged in by persons receiving financial return." Merriam-Webster, last accessed May 1, 2020, https://www.merriam-webster.com/dictionary/professional. A six-year-old selling lemonade on the side of the road is, in the literal sense, also a professional.

So you go see a tax attorney. You tell the tax attorney you would like to reduce those taxes as much as you can. The tax attorney tells you there is something called "tax upstreaming" that could help you.

He knows you are going to need to market your business, and he creates two hypothetical examples for you.

Under scenario one, you set up a California LLC and do your marketing in-house. You film YouTube videos, write a blog, share posts on Facebook, and even purchase some ads on Facebook and Google. Doing it this way in your first year of business, you spend very little on marketing and end the year with $250,000 in revenue and $200,000 in expenses, leaving $50,000 profit.

You are filing taxes on the calendar year (January through December). So in January, that $50,000 passes down onto your 1040 for tax purposes, and you have to pay it at your ordinary income tax rate, which we'll say is 24 percent for federal[2] and 13.3 percent for California. So of the $50,000 profit, $18,650 goes toward taxes, and the rest stays in your bank account for next year.

Under scenario two, instead of doing your marketing in-house, you hire a marketing company based in Nevada, where there is no income tax. The Nevada entity is a corporation that files taxes fiscally, from July to June. At the end of the year, when you see you have about $50,000 in profit, you pay that to the Nevada marketing company to market for you over the next year. Now you've got no profit in California, which means no taxes on the money left in your account at the end of the year.

Because the Nevada corporation pays taxes for income from July to June, it now has six months to use that money to market for you. Let's say at the end of June, the Nevada corporation has spent $30,000 in marketing. It has $20,000 left over, and that gets taxed at the flat federal income tax rate of 21 percent, which is $4,200. It pays nothing in state income tax because Nevada doesn't have state income tax.

---

2. Which would apply to a single filer making between $85,526 and $163,300 for the 2020 tax year.

Under scenario one, you had $50,000 in profit that you paid $18,650 toward state and federal taxes at the end of the year. Under scenario two, you paid no taxes on that $50,000, but you also spent all of your profit, so that hardly seems much of an improvement.

But what if that Nevada corporation, the one doing marketing for you, were *your* corporation? And why not? The tax attorney explains to you that you can set up a Nevada marketing corporation, and all that marketing that you were going to do in-house, you can now pay the marketing corporation to do. Now the marketing corporation is going to be the one purchasing Facebook and Google ads, video production, etc., instead of your California business.

So what does scenario three look like? The California LLC's $50,000 profit at the end of the calendar year gets paid to the Nevada marketing corporation. So while you'll still have to pay taxes on your income in California, you at least won't have to pay any taxes on the $50,000 in profit. Now your Nevada marketing corporation has six months that you didn't have with the California LLC to go use that money to grow the California LLC. At the end of six months, it has spent $30,000 on marketing and pays $4,200 in taxes.

What's the difference between the two scenarios now? In scenario one, you paid $18,650 in taxes. In scenario three, you paid $4,200 in taxes, had another six months of business expenses to further reduce your tax burden, and still have $15,800 left that can be used for marketing in the next fiscal year. And you didn't have to spend any money you wouldn't have spent anyway. This is tax upstreaming.

When your tax attorney finishes explaining this plan to you, you tell him you want to move forward. He recommends you hire a Nevada corporate transactional attorney to set up the Nevada entity and then sends you a bill for $1,500.

You consult with a corporate transactional attorney and try to explain tax upstreaming to her. You want her to set up a Nevada corporation for you that files taxes fiscally from July to June. She knows exactly how to do that but has a lot of questions for you about the tax upstreaming—she wants to make sure she does it right. You aren't sure of all the answers, so you give her the name of your tax attorney.

After your tax attorney and corporate transactional attorney talk, they both want to talk to you. They tell you that there are some things they disagree about. The corporate transactional attorney insists that the corporate bylaws must include certain language, but the tax attorney says that will invalidate some upstreaming advantages.

You aren't sure what to do, so you consult your friend, a litigator who has experience unraveling businesses and getting at personal assets. She tells you that she's not familiar with upstreaming but that you definitely want to make sure there is no mandatory distribution clause or pro rata distribution clause. That could disrupt the charging order protection otherwise available to owners of a Nevada corporation.

In the meantime, you get a bill for $600 from your corporate transactional attorney and another $600 from your tax attorney. You're hesitant to call either of them with this new information because you know it will cost you a lot. For now, you decide to put this on the back burner and focus on your business.

At the beginning of the following year, when it's time to file your taxes, you send your receipts to your CPA and cross your fingers, hoping for the best. Your CPA is quick to deliver the bad news. With all the state and federal taxes that apply to you, you owe a lot of money. You start to research different exemptions that might apply to you and mention them to your CPA. After readjusting the figures, he has reduced your tax burden by about 15 percent, but it is still way higher than you're comfortable with.

You feel a little resentment that you had to go find the deductions. Isn't that what your CPA is supposed to be doing?

Now you're wondering whether you should have moved forward with your tax attorney's plan. You ask your CPA about it, and he tells you that's not something you can do.

You call your tax attorney, and after attempting three times, you finally get a hold of him. You spend several minutes reminding him what your situation is and what recommendations he had made for you. You tell him you are really interested in saving money in taxes, but your CPA says tax upstreaming is not legitimate.

The tax attorney sighs and goes through tax streaming with you again. He says if the CPA says it can't be done, that just means the CPA doesn't know how to do it. He recommends you look for a new CPA.

But your CPA is an old friend and has been doing your taxes for years. Moreover, between your business and personal taxes, you only spend $700 per year to get your taxes filed.

When you get a bill from your tax attorney for $350, you are reminded about how much it cost you just to run the rounds with several professionals.

At this point, you do one of two things: you pay your corporate attorney, your tax attorney, and your estate planning attorney to follow through with each of their recommendations. Among the three of them (and lots of communication amidst disagreements), you spend thousands of dollars setting up an entity with all the right trappings. In the end, if it's done right, it's worth it because of all the tax savings you'll experience year after year. You really hope it's done right. With all the back and forth among the attorneys, you're not sure if what you have is more like the transactional version of Frankenstein's monster.

Alternatively, you end up suffering from analysis paralysis and doing nothing. You just keep using the same CPA. He's comfortable. He's predictable. And although you know you're spending too much in taxes, at least he's cheap.

And ultimately, it's scenarios like this that form a big part of the reason you aren't doing the right thing when it comes to tax structuring. Each professional is familiar with their sphere, but they are largely ignorant of the effects their work has on the other financial aspects of your life. Your estate planning attorney may tie up your assets as tight as a drum so that no creditor can ever touch them. But then you lose control of your assets, which defeats the purpose.

Your corporate transactional attorney may provide maximum corporate liability protection while opening you up to a massive tax hit. In the meantime, your CPA is telling you to buy a new car every year to reduce your taxable income, which does indeed save you almost $10,000 every year in taxes, but only if you purchase a $50,000 vehicle.

When you have multiple professionals, and you want to dip your toe into each of their respective pools, you're just going to end up wet. You'll have a lot of expensive "stuff" that doesn't communicate with each other and may or may not be doing you any good. If a question comes up one year, you have to make the rounds again so you can ensure you're doing everything right. But you just end up spending thousands of dollars again without getting any answers you're confident in.

That, ultimately is the problem. When there are so many different voices, and they're all only looking at part of the problem, you're never getting a complete solution.

When there are so many different voices, and they're all only looking at part of the problem, you're never getting a complete solution.

That plan works just fine for some.
As long as they never make money, get audited, or retire.
There has to be a better way.

PART III
A BETTER WAY

CHAPTER 12

TAX PLANNING V. TAX EVASION

"Over and over again courts have said that there is nothing sinister in so arranging one's affairs as to keep taxes as low as possible. Everybody does so, rich or poor; and all do right, for nobody owes any public duty to pay more than the law demands: taxes are enforced exactions, not voluntary contributions. To demand more in the name of morals is mere cant."

— JUDGE LEARNED HAND

IF YOU HAVE ANY FINANCIAL GOALS, you undoubtedly have one that relates to increasing your income. But that doesn't do you much good if you can't hold on to it. You should have at least one goal to radically reduce the amount of taxes you have to pay during your earning years, and especially during retirement, without having to engage in nonsensical strategies like making unnecessary purchases to qualify for a tax deduction.

When some people hear statements like that, they don't want anything to do with what they consider "tax evasion." But there is something very different between tax structuring and tax planning on the one hand, and tax evasion or tax fraud on the other. Tax evasion and tax fraud are crimes resulting from people hiding money, lying on their returns, or otherwise trying to cheat.

Tax structuring and tax planning are strategies used to play within the government's rules.

Imagine you are playing a game of Monopoly. You land on St. Charles Place, which has a cost of $140. You don't want to purchase it, so you end your turn. Another player, Samantha, says she would like to purchase it for ten dollars. You insist that if she wants to purchase it, she has to land on it. So she opens the rules and shows you this one:

Whenever you land on an unowned property you may buy that property from the Bank at its printed price. You receive the Title Deed card showing ownership; place it face up in front of you.

If you do not wish to buy the property, the Banker sells it at auction to the highest bidder. The buyer pays the Bank the amount of the bid in cash and receives the Title Deed card for that property. Any player, including the one who declined the option to buy it at the printed price, may bid. Bidding may start at any price.[1]

You have been playing Monopoly your entire life and never knew this. In your shock, you don't bid any higher, and Samantha purchases the property for ten dollars. You claim it isn't fair, so she tells you she would be happy to sell it to you for $120—twenty dollars under list price.

You explain that even if you wanted to, you couldn't, because players can't sell properties to one another. She shows you this rule:

Unimproved properties, railroads and utilities (but not buildings) may be sold to any player as a private transaction for any amount the owner can get; however, no property can be sold to another player if buildings are standing on any properties of that color-group.[2]

You realize that you've never actually read the rules and were playing wrong your whole life.

It is now Steve's turn. He rolls two twos. After his turn, he goes again. He gets an extra turn for rolling doubles. Again, he rolls two twos. After his turn, he goes again. Then a third time, he rolls two twos. He moves his token when Samantha tells him that three doubles in a row means he has to go to jail. He doesn't believe her, so she shows him this rule:

---

1. Monopoly, Hasbro.com, last accessed May 21, 2020. https://www.hasbro.com/common/instruct/monins.pdf.
2. *Id.*

If you throw doubles, you move your token as usual, the sum of the two dice, and are subject to any privileges or penalties pertaining to the space on which you land. Retaining the dice, throw again and move your token as before. If you throw doubles three times in succession, move your token immediately to the space marked "In Jail" (see JAIL).[3]

Again, you are impressed by Samantha's knowledge of the rules. But you are also suspicious. Rolling the same combination three times in a row? The chances of that happening are one in 46,656.[4] You inspect the dice and realize that they're weighted. You roll them a few times, and they always land the same way.

Steve was cheating. He was trying to win by operating outside the rules. Samantha was not. She learned the rules and was using them to her advantage.

It's the same with the tax code (or any other law). There is a long and complicated rulebook—one written by multiple authors over more than a hundred years ago. If you know the rules and play within it, you'll have a huge advantage. If you try to break the rules, that's illegal.

There is a long and complicated rulebook—one written by multiple authors over more than a hundred years ago. If you know the rules and play within it, you'll have a huge advantage. If you try to break the rules, that's illegal.

Curiously, even our lawmakers—as well intentioned as they might be[5]—don't fully understand the tax code. Remember how the 401(k) came to be? It

---

3. *Id.*
4. There are thirty-six possible combinations of dice rolls. Two twos is one of them. Every time you roll the dice, you have a $1/36$ chance of getting two twos. Doing it three times in a row is $1/36 \times 1/36 \times 1/36$, or $1/46,646$.
5. With emphasis on the "might."

took a couple of years after the passage of that amendment to really understand how it could be used, which was not how it was originally contemplated.[6]

Although we may recognize the necessity of taxes, no one likes paying them, and no one voluntarily pays more than they are asked to pay. The government does not expect them to. The United States Supreme Court in 1873 illustrated this point well. It had to determine whether a mining and drilling company that was using creative means to lower its tax burden was guilty of the crime of tax evasion.

Finding nothing wrong with the way the company had structured their taxes, the Supreme Court used an example of the Stamp Act of 1862 to illustrate. The Stamp Act imposed a tax of two cents for every bank check written for at least twenty dollars. The Supreme Court explained that if a man chose to write two checks for ten dollars each instead of writing one check for twenty dollars, he still pays his creditor, but he owes no stamp tax. The court concluded, "While his operations deprive the government of the duties it might reasonably expect to receive, it is not perceived that the practice is open to the charge of fraud. He resorts to devices to avoid the payment of duties, but they are not illegal. He has the legal right to split up his evidences of payment, and thus to avoid the tax."[7]

Another court considering a similar issue reached the same conclusion: "We do not speak of evasion, because, when the law draws a line, a case is on one side of it or the other, and if on the safe side is none the worse legally that a party has availed himself to the full of what the law permits."[8]

Unfortunately, navigating the tax code is no easy feat. To try to figure out what one can do or not do within the bounds of the law is something that stumped even one of the greatest minds who ever lived. Indeed, when asked for his reaction to a labyrinth of income tax questions, Albert Einstein was perplexed: "This is a question too difficult for a mathematician. It should be asked of a philosopher."

6. See discussion at page 12.
7. *United States v. Isham*, 84 U.S. 496, 506, 21 L. Ed. 728 (1873).
8. *Bullen v. State of Wisconsin*, 240 U.S. 625, 630, 36 S. Ct. 473, 474, 60 L. Ed. 830 (1916).

The tax code is an ever-evolving piece of legislation. It's a moving target. But that doesn't mean you can't learn to be an exceptionally good sharpshooter.

The tax code is an ever-evolving piece of legislation. It's a moving target. But that doesn't mean you can't learn to be an exceptionally good sharpshooter.

Armed with the right knowledge, you don't have to let the tax code strangle you. You can unshackle yourself. You can take control of your own future by eliminating (or significantly reducing) your *taxable* retirement income and funding your retirement with *nontaxable* income.

CHAPTER 13

ATTRIBUTES OF THE PERFECT INVESTMENT VEHICLE

"It's not how much money you make, but how much money you keep, how hard it works for you, and how many generations you keep it for."
—Robert Kiyosaki

AT THIS POINT IN THE BOOK, if you've been paying attention, you should have some serious reservations about putting any more money into the government's annuity account that they've labeled a 401(k), IRA, SEP, etc.

But what is the alternative? What would it look like?

Let's take the lessons we've learned to paint a picture of that perfect investment vehicle.

LESSONS WE LEARNED FROM THE 401(K)

A 401(k) is not so much an investment as it is an investment vehicle, or tax wrapper. When you buy real estate, stocks, or bonds, that is an investment. When you put money in a 401(k), that money is not "invested" in the 401(k). It is invested in mutual funds and subject to the tax rules in section 401(k) of the tax code.

With most 401(k)s, you are severely limited in what you can actually invest—both because of limitations imposed by the tax rules and because of the limited options the investment broker makes available to you (usually mutual funds). Accordingly, it may feel like putting money in your 401(k) is the same as putting it in the mutual fund, but the 401(k) is not the investment—it's just the tax wrapper for the investment. The mutual fund is the actual investment.

Regardless of *what* you invest in, you want the investment vehicle, or the tax wrapper for the investment, to be the most advantageous to you. The 401(k), which we have already discussed at length, is part of the government's revenue-generation plan and is *not* the best tax wrapper for your investment.

We know from our study of the 401(k) that the government, through our "contract" with them, places many restrictions on the money in the beginning, the middle, and the end. But what would it look like if we didn't voluntarily put our money in a place with all those restrictions? Let's take a look.

The Perfect Investment Vehicle Would Allow You Freedom to Invest When, How Much, and How Long You Want

When you invest in a 401(k), you are doing it on the government's terms, and you're agreeing to abide by any new terms the government comes up with. It's that target that moves even as you try to hit it. Remember, with a 401(k), you can only invest up to the annual contribution limit, which is $19,500 if you're single and younger than fifty years old. For an IRA, that limit is $6,000. That amount regularly changes, and whatever the new amounts are, you'll be subject to them.

The limits to how long you can invest are also always potentially in flux. Prior to 2020, you could only contribute to an IRA through age 70½. For now, there is no upper age limit. To contribute to a 401(k), you have to be employed with an employer that offers one. Otherwise, you're out of luck.

The perfect investment vehicle would have no such restrictions. It will allow you to contribute as much as you want without any arbitrary, one-size-fits-all, government-imposed contributions limits. It would allow you to contribute regardless of whether your employer offers a plan or whether you are employed at all. It would also allow you to pay for it as long (or as short) as you want.

The Perfect Investment Vehicle Would Allow You to Invest in Anything You Want

These qualified-plan tax wrappers don't just determine how much taxes you are going to pay on your investment. They also tell you what you're allowed to invest in.

For example, you cannot use your money to invest in derivative trades, antiques or collectibles, and most real estate.[1] If you want to invest in coins, you can, but only if it is a certain type of coin like the Canadian Maple Leaf or the American Gold Buffalo coins. With a traditional IRA, you cannot borrow money from it, sell property to it, use it as collateral for a loan, or use it to purchase property for personal use.[2]

The perfect investment vehicle would not have any such restrictions. It would allow you to invest your money in anything you want: mutual funds, rare art, all coins, real estate, or that rare Boba Fett action figure. It would also allow you to use your investment money to pay off debt, start up a business, or as collateral for a loan. It would have no prohibited transactions at all.

Remember the casino chip analogy?[3] Our perfect investment is not going to require us to trade in our cash for chips that are only good for certain things. Our perfect investment is going to be more like cash—you can spend it on anything you want.

The Perfect Investment Vehicle Would Protect Against Loss of Your Principal

Recall that most 401(k)s and other qualified accounts are usually built on mutual funds, which are just a combination of different securities—stocks,

---

1. Publication 590-A (2019), 26 U.S.C. § 4975, IRS, last accessed May 4, 2020, https://www. irs.gov/publications/p590a#en_US_2018_publink1000230870 (once at this page, click on the link for "Prohibited Transactions" in the table of contents).
2. *Id.*
3. See the discussion on page 40.

bonds, money market instruments, etc. You've heard the phrase "diversify your portfolio." That's what a mutual fund is doing.

Instead of buying one hundred dollars of Amazon stock and living or dying with Amazon, a mutual fund will buy two dollars of Amazon stock, two dollars of Apple stock, fifteen dollars in government-backed bonds, etc. If one stock does really poorly, your fund could still grow based on the performance of the other stocks.

Of course, the converse is also true. A stock that is performing really well could be undermined by the rest of your fund doing poorly. Mutual funds are not immune to market fluctuations. When the entire market is doing poorly, most mutual funds will too.

That's where that 43 percent drop in the market every 9.875 years comes into play.[4]

All this is to say that when you put your retirement savings—your future income—into mutual funds held in a 401(k) tax wrapper, you're gambling with your future. You are subjecting your future lifestyle to the volatility of the market.

The perfect investment vehicle is not going to subject something so important as your income to market volatility. In fact, the perfect investment would come with a guarantee that your principal will never be lost—that every penny you put into it will be there until you want to pull it out.

The Perfect Investment Vehicle Would Not Be Subject to Unknowable Future Taxes

One of the worst parts of your deal with the government, the one called the 401(k), is the open-ended nature of the taxes. Taxes will have to be paid on 100 percent of the money in the 401(k) tax wrapper whether you outlive it or not. We just don't know what that tax rate will be.

---

4. See the discussion on pages 54–55.

What we do know is that the government keeps going deeper and deeper in debt and that tax rates are at a historical low at the writing of this book. So ask yourself what's more likely: (1) the government learns to manage its money with more prudence so they can pay off their debt with the money they have,[5] or (2) it raises taxes?

What's more likely: (1) the government learns to manage its money with more prudence so they can pay off their debt with the money they have, or (2) it raises taxes?

If you're like every other person to whom I have ever asked this question, your answer is either number two or some combination of number two and number one. I'm not sure there is a red-blooded American alive who thinks the government will somehow figure out what it has never been able to do before and start living within its means.

Whatever happens—whatever the tax rate becomes, if you've got money in a qualified plan, you're going to have to pay taxes.

The perfect investment vehicle, on the other hand, would not give the government a blank check. There would not be any unknowable and open tax rate to be unilaterally determined by a government deep in debt.

In fact, since we're talking *perfect* investment vehicle, it wouldn't be taxed at all. Its growth would not be taxed, and neither would the money you use before or during retirement.

---

5. If there is any part of this book you find humorous, it should be this.

The Perfect Investment Vehicle Would Be Liquid Immediately and Give You the Freedom to Withdraw As Much of It as You Want Whenever You Want

With the 401(k), your money is not liquid. Using your money before the government says you can requires you to abandon 10 percent of it and pay taxes. But once those investments have had time to grow, the government wants to start collecting taxes, and the government's patience is not infinite. So, once you reach age seventy-two, if you haven't started paying taxes on all that accumulation, the government is going to force you to. They do that through the innocuous-sounding required minimum distributions.

The perfect investment vehicle, on the other hand, would recognize what the 401(k) does not—that it is *your* money. So there would be no penalties for accessing it and no restrictions on how long or short you can invest it.

You want to use the money now to repair the leaks on your roof? Here it is. Want to leave it to grow until you are seventy-five? Yes, you can. Want to do anything else with it now, soon, later, much later, or never? No problem.

The Perfect Investment Vehicle Would Have Definite Terms with a Predictable Future, and If a Contract, Would Give You Enforceable Rights

Remember, we're talking about your money and your future. There should be predictability and definiteness so you can plan. Whereas the 401(k) is a big illusory promise with no commitment from the government about what rules they'll create for your money in the future and along the way,[6] the perfect investment vehicle has to come to the table and match your commitments with its own: you should know exactly what you're agreeing to before you spend or invest any of your money.

---

6. See the discussion starting on page 17.

What kind of interest rate can you expect? How much can you contribute? How long can you contribute? How much flexibility is there in the contribution amount? How accessible is the money? What can it be used for? How long can I leave it in there?

In fact, just like any other financial transaction (except those with the government), the terms should be something the perfect investment vehicle is willing to put in writing, sign, and be bound to—an actual contract.

> *Just like any other financial transaction (except those with the government), the terms should be something the perfect investment vehicle is willing to put in writing, sign, and be bound to—an actual contract.*

The Perfect Investment Vehicle Would Not Just Be Yours in Name; It Would Be Property Legally and Legitimately Owned by You

Recall that our analysis of property law left us wondering if the money in a 401(k) is even ours, considering that we give up pretty much every right of ownership when we contribute to it.[7] Those five rights of ownership—possession, control, exclusion, enjoyment, and disposition—are abandoned, either in whole or in part.

The perfect investment vehicle would require no such sacrifice. It would be like any other property we own. We may give up part of a right here or there in exchange for a benefit. For example, we may give someone else the right to possess and control the money in exchange for growth on our money (like investing in a business), or we may temporarily give up our disposition rights to create something better (like pledging it as collateral

---

7. See the discussion starting on page 37.

135

for a loan). But we're not giving up *all* rights, and those we are leveraging are being leveraged on our terms.

There have to be at least two major differences between the 401(k) and the perfect investment vehicle when it comes to property rights: (1) we aren't going to be giving them all away, and (2) whatever we do must be revocable: it's our money, and if we want, we can take our money and go home.

CHAPTER 14

THE INVESTMENT GRADE INSURANCE CONTRACT

"Give me six hours to chop down a tree and I will spend the first four sharpening the axe."

— Abraham Lincoln

LET ME INTRODUCE YOU to the best investment vehicle you've never heard of: the investment grade insurance contract.

The investment grade insurance contract, or IGIC™, is exactly what it sounds like. It's an insurance contract set up to be an investment vehicle.

But what exactly does that mean? Let's take a closer look.

A BRIEF HISTORY OF INSURANCE

Insurance is not exactly a sexy topic at dinner parties. Its history is not something you learn at school, not something you've ever looked up on your own, and probably not something you're too interested in now, so I'll keep this brief, and with luck, even a little interesting.

Insurance in its simplest form is a strategy for spreading out risk so when calamity comes, no single person has to bear the brunt of loss. It has been around in some form for thousands of years.

Insurance, as we're familiar with it, traces its roots to seventeenth-century England.[1] The Great Fire of London in 1666 destroyed tens of thousands of

---

1. Whit Thompson, "How Insurance Began: 3,000 Years of History," WSR Blog, September 13, 2016, last accessed July 8, 2020, http://wsrinsurance.com/how-insurance-began-3000-years-of-history.

homes. As a result, an entrepreneurial man named Nicholas Barbon built a fire insurance business.[2]

Ben Franklin started a fire insurance company in the 1750s.[3] Life insurance was born in the 1800s.[4]

Modern insurance, at its core, is an indemnity contract between the insurer and the insured.[5] In simple terms, the insured's contractual obligations consist of making regular payments to the insurer, called "premiums." In exchange, the insurer promises to indemnify, or pay for, covered losses up to the agreed-upon coverage amount.

Life insurance is similar. You, the insurer, pay premiums. If you die within the coverage period, the life insurance company pays to whomever you have designated, called "beneficiary(ies)," the agreed-upon coverage amount, called the "death benefit."

Life insurance was envisioned as a way for families to be able to take care of themselves when the primary breadwinner passes away. Thus, the death benefit for this type of insurance is calculated by taking the number of years in an income-earner's work-life expectancy, multiplying it by their expected average annual income, and then reducing it to present value.

Thus, if a forty-year-old income earner expects to work to age sixty-five (another twenty-five years), and anticipates making an average of $100,000 per year, the needed death benefit will be calculated at $2.5 million, or twenty-five years times $100,000.[6] Because this was replacing the value of a life, it has never been taxed.

2. Id.
3. Id.
4. Id.
5. Meyer v. Bldg. & Realty Serv. Co., 209 Ind. 125, 134, 196 N.E. 250, 253–54 (1935) ("Insurance has been defined as a contract whereby one undertakes to indemnify another against loss, damage, or liability arising from an unknown or contingent event.")
6. That number is sometimes reduced to present value, which takes into account that $2.5 million now is worth more than $100,000 over 25 years because it can grow over time. This is the principle known as "time value of money."

This is term insurance—where the insurance coverage is limited to a specified term. In our example, it may be a twenty-five-year term. For the next twenty-five working years, if the insured dies, the death benefit will be paid. But if the insured survives, the term policy expires, and presumably, the family will be taken care of from retirement or pension funds if the breadwinner dies during retirement.[7]

Term insurance is inexpensive if the insured is young because a huge majority (around 98 percent) outlive their policy, so they never pay out.[8] As one gets older, the cost of term insurance increases exponentially as they near the age where death becomes more certain. Of those who purchase term insurance, 100 percent will die either before or after the term expires (according to those really smart actuaries working for insurance companies). In other words, death is a certainty. It's the timing we're not sure of.

Permanent Life Insurance

Life insurance has become much more than just insurance against death. Many insurance contracts also have a cash value component to them, which means that part of your premium goes to pay for the death benefit, and part of your premium goes into a cash account. The insurance company pays a competitive and guaranteed interest rate on money in the cash account. Plus, depending on the company's earnings, they typically will pay a nonguaranteed dividend, which also contributes to the growth of the cash account.

Many of these policies with cash value are permanent. Unlike term, which is temporary insurance that lapses after a specified time period, permanent insurance has a guaranteed death benefit payout as long as the insured is not in breach of the contract (which usually just means the premiums are current).

---

7. We presume this because it would be terribly poor planning to only get insurance that is set to expire without having any other way to provide for your family.
8. William Scott Page, "The Life Insurance Industry's Big Secret," HuffPost, December 4, 2012, last accessed July 8, 2020, https://www.huffpost.com/entry/the-life-insurance-indust_b.

One of the best features of this cash account is that it is asset protected, which means your creditors can't get at it, and it maintains a tax-privileged status (no taxes!). These protections are not unlimited (it's a state-by-state thing). We'll get into the specifics of that later.

Throughout the last two centuries, millions of people have taken advantage of whole-life cash-value-driven insurance contracts. They would stuff all their cash into a life insurance contract where it could grow tax free and be creditor protected.

The problem was, someone could have a whole lot of cash value with a relatively small death benefit. Because it was technically an insurance contract, they would get all the tax protections of insurance even though it was more like a large savings and investment account.

Congress perceived this as an abuse,[9] and in amendments passed in 1984 and 1988, defined life insurance statutorily for the first time. This placed limits on how much cash could be put into a life insurance contract.[10]

The definition and rules are complicated. In essence, to qualify as a life insurance contract (and get all the tax and investment benefits associated with the insurance contract), the ratio of cash value to death benefit cannot be too high (as determined by the statutory test), and the premiums have to be spread out over time.[11] As long as it meets the test, it meets the definition of insurance contract. If the ratio is too high, it permanently morphs into a "modified endowment contract," or MEC (pronounced "mech"), and it loses the special tax status that life insurance contracts enjoy.

In response to this change in insurance taxation rules, insurance companies have adapted. They have created products designed to maximize that allowable cash-value-to-death-benefit ratio so consumers can still take advantage of

---

9. H.R. Rep. No. 432, 98th Cong., 2d Sess. 102 (1983).
10. You'll find these changes as part of the existing tax code at 26 U.S.C. § 7702 and 26 U.S.C. § 101.
11. This is a very simplified explanation of a very complicated formula. Go read § 7702 of the tax code if you want to try to decipher the complicated version.

ZACHARIAH B. PARRY

the huge tax advantages of a life insurance contract without crossing the line into what Congress considers a MEC. (That's where it pays to read the rules before you start playing the game.)

Permanent insurance contracts can be written up in an infinite number of ways. With variabilities possible with insurance carriers, premium ratios, riders, growth basis, and dividend allocations, no two contracts are the same, and not all are created equal. Different types of insurance contracts serve different purposes, and some are a bad deal altogether.

Unfortunately, life insurance has gotten a bit of a bad rap. Have you ever met a life insurance agent that you wanted to hang out with again?[12]

And it's no wonder. I've heard of life insurance agents, desperate to close that sale, using this line: "You want to provide for your family if you die, don't you? You don't want your wife to have to become a stripper to pay the bills, do you?"

Popular radio personality Dave Ramsey has never pulled punches when it comes to whole-life policies: "There is never a good time to be saving money inside one of those rip-off whole-life, cash value insurance plans. They are bad plans."[13]

Of course, if your purpose is to temporarily insure a life through income replacement (death benefit), and you aren't concerned at all about taxes or retirement, then Ramsey is absolutely right. Term insurance is the way to go.

You can do what other financially ignorant people do and *plan* to "buy term and then invest the rest." Then you *actually* buy term and not invest the difference. Or invest it somewhere that will ultimately kill you in taxes. Retirement isn't for everyone.

Also, keep in mind that if your agent doesn't set up your insurance contract correctly, it really can be a rip-off. Some plans are tied to the stock market and

---

12. Maybe, but there is a reason Ned Ryerson's (Stephen Tobolowsky) character on *Groundhog Day* was such a great satirical bit. There was so much truth in it. And who can't relate to Phil Connors's (Bill Murray) reaction to the life insurance pitch?
13. Dave Ramsey, "How Do I Close My Whole Life Insurance Policy?" Daveramsey.com, last visited July 8, 2020, https://www.daveramsey.com/askdave/insurance/closing-whole-life.

promise huge potential gains with no potential losses. They're really not that different than mere mutual funds with a continually renewing (and exponential increases in costs) term policies. Other permanent policies have long vesting periods with steep surrender penalties.

But if your purpose is to find an asset-protected, tax-free retirement vehicle with a guaranteed rate of return and a guarantee against loss of your principle (and a whole lot more), you can do no better than a properly created whole life policy.

If it's created a particular way, including maximizing the cash-value-to-death-benefit ratio, and acts as a tax wrapper for your investments (*tax-free wrapper!*), it is a special type of whole life policy called an investment grade insurance contract (IGIC).

But does the IGIC check all the boxes of the perfect investment vehicle, i.e., is it functionally the opposite of a 401(k)? Let's review. Remember, our perfect investment vehicle is going to have the following attributes:

- allows freedom to invest when, how much, and how long you want
- allows you to invest in anything you want
- protects against loss of your principal
- is not subject to unknowable future taxes
- is liquid immediately with freedom to withdraw as much of it as you want whenever you want
- provides options for employee carve outs
- gives definite terms with a predictable future, and if a contract, gives you enforceable rights
- allows property to be legally and legitimately owned by you

Allows freedom to invest when, how much, and how long you want

The IGIC is completely flexible. You get to set the terms. You can decide how much you want to put away without respect to any arbitrary government-imposed contribution limits. The only upper limits are to the death benefit and correspond to how insurable you are. But since we're maximizing the cash-value-to-death-benefit ratio, often those limits are well above what people can afford or are willing to pay. In any case, they are much higher than the contribution caps on qualified accounts.

The IGIC is also extremely flexible regarding how long you want to pay. In some cases, you can set it up so your contract is fully paid up in as little as two years. That means it is fully funded, the death benefit is guaranteed, and you never have to pay another premium. The principal will grow inside the insurance contract, but you can also set it up to grow outside the contract.

On the long end, again, if it is set up right, you can pay for as long as you want.[14] Many insurance contracts have an upper limit of 121 years old, but considering that very few people in history have ever lived to be that old, that won't be a problem for all but the record-breakers for life longevity.

Allows you to invest in anything you want

With the 401(k), there are prohibited investment transactions. But most 401(k) "owners" are just picking one of a handful of the most popular mutual funds. (i.e., the ones suggested by the financial planner). I imagine most 401(k) contributors don't feel particularly constrained by the prohibited transaction rules because they don't realize they could have options.

If you put your money in a 401(k), you'll have a sit-down with a financial planner, and they will have you answer a few questions about your goals and risk tolerance. Then they will hand you a packet with several mutual funds that they say fit your goals. You point to one, sign a few documents, and then you start contributing paycheck after paycheck, feeling good about the fact that you are saving for retirement.

---

14. In some circumstances, paying too much for too long will cause it to become a modified endowment contract. But if you anticipate your expected contributions, the policy can be written in a way that it won't ever MEC (exceed the tax law limits).

If you put your money into an IGIC, you become the master of your own destiny.

If you put your money into an IGIC, you become the master of your own destiny. If mutual funds are your thing, then by all means, seek out a financial planner. If you prefer investing in real estate, do it. Venture capitalism. Cryptocurrency. Collectibles. You can invest in your own business, someone else's business, or no business at all. You can use the money for emergencies, to pay off debt, to remodel your house. There are no limitations.

Protects against loss of your principal

With a 401(k), your money is tied to the market (less the fees that get taken out). So if the market does well enough to beat the fees, then you do well too. But if the market corrects, which it regularly does, you suffer the consequences. There is simply no guarantee that the funds in your 401(k) are safe. Or that they will grow. The one big certainty is taxes.

With an IGIC, your principal is guaranteed against loss. Further, it is guaranteed to grow at a contractually guaranteed interest rate. This means there is an actual commitment. In writing.

Herein lies one of the biggest advantages of the IGIC as an investment vehicle vs. the 401(k). As an investment *vehicle*, the 401(k) doesn't actually do anything but restrict what you can do and promise to tax you later. A 401(k) is not an organization that does anything with your money. It's just a code designed to take your money. With that tax wrapper, you stick your money in the hands of a brokerage firm who makes money off your money even if you don't.

But the IGIC as an investment vehicle is different. The IGIC is typically going to be held by a mutual insurance company,[15] and it's going to grow inside the contract. If all you ever do is make contributions and let

---

15. A mutual insurance company is much different than a mutual fund.

your cash value grow, you can at least count on compound growth. Growth. Not loss. Guaranteed.

But that's just growth inside the contract. If you want (and you should), you can use the money you've accumulated to invest outside the contract. You do this by using the cash value as collateral for a loan. Then with the loan, which you aren't paying penalties or taxes on—just interest—you can invest in anything you want.[16] Or pay bills. Or buy a car.

The best part is, if the IGIC is set up right and you use it right, the growth in the policy is always going to exceed the interest accruing on the loan. As a result, even when you borrow, you're earning money. It's like getting paid to take out a loan.

Is not subject to unknowable future taxes

As you'll recall, when you contribute to a 401(k), you are writing the government a blank check and promising to pay taxes at whatever rate they choose at the time you start withdrawing.

When you are contributing to an IGIC, you are using *after-tax* dollars to contribute. You do not get a tax deduction on your contribution like you would with the 401(k). With an IGIC, you are telling the government, "I am going to pay my taxes now at this known rate so I never have to pay taxes on this money (or its growth) again." So because you've already paid your taxes, when it comes time to use that money during retirement, it's tax free. And that's huge.

The difference between being taxed and not being taxed makes a sizeable difference in retirement. Let's say you have one million dollars in your retirement account. You receive $1,500 per month in Social Security, and you need a total of $10,000 per month to maintain your lifestyle. Consider the difference in taking income on a taxed versus a nontaxed basis:

---

16. Interest accrues on the loan, but you don't necessarily have to be the one who pays it. You can set it up so your death benefit does that after you die. More on that later.

If you have to pay taxes on the money you withdraw, you're going to have to withdraw more than $10,000 monthly to be left with $10,000 in your pocket. Because you've got $1,500 in Social Security income, you need your 401(k) (your taxable account) to provide an additional $8,500 monthly. If your annual 401(k) income is $102,000 per year, that puts you in the 24 percent tax bracket.[17]

Because of our progressive tax system, figuring out how much you need to pull out over one year to pay those taxes is a little complicated. But I've done the math for you. That magic number is $126,223.80.[18]

If you could keep all of your Social Security income, that would be the end of the analysis. You would withdraw $126,223.80 from your 401(k) ($10,518.65 per month), pay $24,223.80 in taxes annually ($2,018.65 for every month's withdrawal), and end up with $8,500 per month from the 401(k) and $1,500 from Social Security.

However, you have exceeded the Social Security tax threshold, which varies based on your marital and tax filing status. At over $100,000, you're well over double the highest threshold. So, you have to pay taxes on 85 percent of your Social Security, too. Since your total Social Security is $18,000 annually ($1,500 monthly), that 85 percent amounts to $15,300 annually ($1,275 monthly). Since we've already calculated the taxes in your lower brackets, you're going to pay the entire 85 percent at the 24 percent bracketed rate.[19]

Twenty-four percent of $15,300 is $3,672, which seems like the way to calculate how much more you need to withdraw from your 401(k), but that

---

17. We start with the assumption that you won't be taxed on your Social Security income because well, that's what should happen (and what does happen with really low incomes).
18. The first $9,875 is taxed at 10% ($987.50); the next $20,250 is taxed at 12% ($3,630); the next $45,400 is taxed at 22% ($9,988.00), and the last $40,698 is taxed at 24% ($9,618.29). That is a total of $126,223.80 taxed with a total of $24,223.79 in taxes, leaving the $102,000.01 you need to supplement your $18,000 in Social Security for a total of $120,000 annually or $10,000 monthly.
19. Granted, you could still use the standard deduction to lower your income. Most of your other deductions will probably be gone, though. Even so, the standard deduction is not enough to put you even close to below the Social Security threshold, so you're paying tax on 85% of your Social Security regardless.

ZACHARIAH B. PARRY

would leave you short. You also have to pay taxes on that additional money you withdraw. See how the 401(k) is the gift that keeps on giving?

Since $15,300 is 76 percent of what you actually need, to get the other 24 percent, you *divide* $15,300 by 76 percent. That number, $20,131.58, is the total you need so that after 24 percent taxes, you have $15,300 left. This means you must withdraw an additional $4,831.58 from your 401(k) each year ($402.63 per month), so you end up with $10,000 in your pocket every month after taxes.

I know that's a lot of math. Without the math, though, we would never know what we're getting into.

Let me simplify it for you. With a 401(k), to have $10,000 per month to spend toward your lifestyle ($120,000 annually), $1,500 of which comes from Social Security ($18,000 annually), you actually need to withdraw $131,055.38 from your 401(k) ($10,921.28 monthly).

What if you need $10,000 per month and you have an IGIC with $1,000,000 and $1,500 per month in income from Social Security? Well, you borrow $8,500 per month against the total $1,000,000 balance.

That's it. The math is easy because there are no taxes. Because it's only taxable income that counts toward the Social Security taxation, even though you're pulling out $102,000 per year, none of that counts toward the Social Security taxation thresholds, so you get to keep 100 percent of your Social Security too.

In both scenarios, you have $10,000 in monthly spending money. With the 401(k), you're depleting your total retirement by $10,921.28, but with the IGIC, you're only using $8,500 per month. That's a $2,421.28 difference ($29,055.36 annually).

Of course, all of this assumes that you're withdrawing now, not in the future, or that taxes don't change between now and when you retire.

But what happens if, as will undoubtedly happen, taxes are higher in the future?

Our first scenario just gets worse. To hit that $10,000 monthly figure, you're going to have to pull out more money to accommodate the higher tax rate.

Our second scenario, well, it stays exactly the same. When you don't owe taxes (because you've already paid them), it doesn't matter whether the tax rate is 2 percent or 200 percent. Two percent of zero and 200 percent of zero are both zero.

> *When you don't owe taxes (because you've already paid them), it doesn't matter whether the tax rate is 2 percent or 200 percent. Two percent of zero and 200 percent of zero are both zero.*

Is liquid immediately with freedom to withdraw as much of it as you want whenever you want

When you put money in a mutual fund that's been wrapped with those 401(k) tax promises, you are essentially sticking it into a prison cell and handing the key to the government. As Uncle Sam takes the key, he promises you, "When you turn 59½, I'll unlock the door, and you can have your money less my share... unless I decide to keep it longer or let you have it sooner. If you want it any sooner than that, I would be happy to temporarily open the door for you. For a fee."

With the IGIC, you are sticking your money in a cushy, air-conditioned vault. You have the key. Anytime you want to access any of the money, you can get it. You don't have to apply first. You don't have to wait. You don't have to pay. It's your money.

With some permanent policies, there is a vesting period—usually around seven years, before you can access the money without a surrender charge. Seven years is a lot better than waiting until you are 59½ (unless you're fifty-three or older). But with the IGIC, your cash is your cash. You can access it immediately.

Provides options for employee carve outs

If you are an employer, and you offer a 401(k) to your employees, you cannot favor yourself over your employees. The IRS requires "that the contributions

ZACHARIAH B. PARRY

made by and for rank-and-file employees are proportional to contributions made for owners and managers."[20]

That's not true of the IGIC. You can set up an account for you and none for your employees. Or smaller ones for your employees. Or just for your favorite employees. You name it. It's your company. An IGIC is set up through a private company governed by a private contract, and there are no discrimination rules.[21] So go crazy.

Gives definite terms with a predictable future, and if a contract, gives you enforceable rights

Remember when we compared a 401(k) to a contract?[22] If you really understood the exchange of promises in your deal with the government (which is just you promising in exchange for them promising to not promise anything), you would think a lot harder before you put any money into that plan.

On the other hand, an investment grade insurance contract, as the name suggests, is an actual contract. The terms are definite. Many of those terms are negotiable. You know going in exactly what the insurance company is promising.

And what are they promising, exactly?

With an IGIC, they're promising liquidity. They're promising a death benefit. Living benefits. Guarantees against your principle being lost. A guaranteed interest rate.

You know what else? They are also going to throw in some bonuses that aren't part of the promise in the form of dividends.

20. IRS.gov, "401(k) Plan Fix-It Guide - The plan failed the 401(k) ADP and ACP nondiscrimination tests," https://www.irs.gov/retirement-plans/401k-plan-fix-it-guide-the-plan-failed-the-401k-adp-and-acp-nondiscrimination-tests, last accessed May 22, 2020.
21. The word "discrimination" carries heavy connotations. I am using it here not in reference to any protected class: race, gender, nationality, etc. I am using it in the same way you discriminate when you decide whether to have pepperoni or Canadian bacon on your pizza—exercising your freedom to choose.
22. See discussion beginning on page 15.

HACKLED

IGICs are usually facilitated through mutual insurance companies. That means when you sign the insurance contract, you become a co-owner of the company. Therefore, when dividends are issued, you are entitled to them.

Mutual companies don't know how all their assets will perform in the future, so they can't (and don't) guarantee dividends. But they do promise that when there are dividends to be paid, you will get a proportionate share of them based on your policy.

But it gets even better. There are some really good mutual companies out there with a stellar track record for paying dividends. They want to pay dividends. They want a long history of paying dividends. The more dividends they pay and the more often they pay them, the better their reputation, and the more people want to choose them over other mutual companies.

Whereas the government doesn't particularly care if you like their product—they'll take their taxes either way—the mutual companies, like any other private companies, are competing for your business. One of the best ways to attract new business is to show a solid history of dividend performance.

Penn Mutual, for example, in their 173-year history, has paid dividends every single year without fail.[23] Think about that. Penn Mutual was founded in Philadelphia in 1847. James Polk was president. Abraham Lincoln was thirty-eight years old. The Civil War was still fourteen years in the future. Through every financial downturn in the last century plus, including the Great Depression, they have paid a dividend.

Can you think of anything else man-made that has consistently happened for 173 years in a row?

Whereas the government is consistently taking, mutual companies are establishing an amazing record of giving—not because they're contractually bound to do so, but because they know the happier their clients, the more clients they'll get and the better off everyone will be.

23. "2019 Annual Report," Penn Mutual, April 2020, last accessed July 8, 2020, https://www. pennmutual.com/static-assets/annual-report/Penn-Mutual-Annual-Report-2019.pdf.

Allows property to be legally and legitimately owned by you

When you jump on that 401(k) train, you're effectively giving up your property rights in property that you're pretty sure is yours but doesn't really feel like yours at all.[24]

If the 401(k) were a case of beers, they would be locked in a vending machine stored in your broker's office. If you want some, you have to stick your crisp bills and coins in the machine. And unless you want an invoice later, too, you have to clean out the bottle, fill it back up, and put it back in. In the meantime, your broker gets paid to drink your beer.

With an IGIC, the money isn't just yours in name—it's actually yours. You get to choose what to do with it. You can leave it there, borrow against it, take it out. You can sell it if you want.[25]

The topic of ownership rights always reminds me of a story about my dad that has reached legendary status in our family. He was a seventeen-year-old senior at a small high school in Melba, Idaho (where the population has never been greater than a few hundred).

One particular evening, he was in a large potato cellar helping prepare a float for a school parade. There were several other students working together to complete the float. One of them came to my dad and offered him a bottle of beer. My dad, who didn't (and still doesn't) drink, accepted the beer. Then without a word, he flung it at a brick wall where it exploded in a shower of glass and amber liquid.

"What'dya do that for?" his benefactor loudly complained.

"Hey, it's my beer," my dad said with a shrug, simply and calmly, before he turned back to his work.

---

24. See discussion of property rights starting on page 37.
25. You know those commercials you see on TV about selling a life insurance policy? If you have an IGIC, that's a valuable asset. The more mature it is, the more valuable, too valuable for me to want to sell mine, but when you own one, it's yours. You can do what you want with it.

That might not have earned him any points with whoever paid for the beer, but he had a point. And he understood the benefits of property ownership. If you own it, it's yours to do with as you please.

Those funds in the IGIC? You can throw them against the wall if you want. They're yours. They're a case of beer in a mini fridge sitting in your garage. Your garage. Your mini fridge. Your beer.

What's more, because you're putting your money in a mutual company, it's not just your money—it also becomes partly your company. Instead of your ownership rights being diminished (like with a 401[k]), you maintain your ownership rights in your cash value, and you get new ownership rights in the insurance company.

Have you ever owned part of a life insurance company before? I gotta be honest; it feels pretty good.

Social Security and Medicare

Remember, because the Social Security Ponzi scheme is a ticking time bomb waiting to implode,[26] the government needed to recoup some of those losses. So during retirement, once you are taking at least $25,000 of annual taxable income, including your 401(k) income, the government starts taxing your Social Security income too.

What about retirement income from an IGIC? The answer depends on how you take it.

If you just withdraw the money you put in, then you can take that money (which you already paid taxes on), and it doesn't count as income and won't trigger income requirements for Social Security taxation purposes. Once you have taken out the equivalent of what you put in, and you start withdrawing the growth, it counts as ordinary income, is taxed, and counts against you for Social Security taxation.

---

26. See discussion starting on page 63.

However, if instead you fund your retirement using loans against the cash value, that's not income,[27] and you will neither be taxed on it, nor will it trigger taxation on your Social Security.[28] And you don't have to pay the loan back. Your death benefit will. You get to choose how to use your IGIC. Which way are you going to go?

The same is true for premiums for Medicare Part B and D. Funding your retirement from an IGIC doesn't count against you for premium calculations.

Anything Else?

You probably noticed that the last several subsections were basically just a list of opposites. We took all the bad attributes of a 401(k) and then looked at the IGIC to see how it compared, which revealed a lot of freedom and flexibility with the IGIC.

But there is a lot more to an IGIC than just an answer to the 401(k).

For example, a 401(k) does not come with a death benefit, which means that if you want to protect your family against your death, you've got to purchase life insurance separately. What's more, if you were drinking the 401(k) punch, you probably were also of the buy-term-and-invest-the-rest mindset. So you likely are just paying for something that will expire before you use it (that's the best case scenario anyway).

The IGIC, because it is an insurance contract, comes with a death benefit. That death benefit is guaranteed to pay (as long as you keep the premiums up to date and don't live past age 121).

The death benefit has become much more than just income replacement at death, though. With term insurance, the insurance company is counting on you outsurviving the policy. They only make money if they spend less on those who die than they collect on everyone. But with a guaranteed death benefit, the

27. Technically, it's a debt.
28. Read more about how the IGIC works during retirement starting on page 195.

insurance company has figured out how to make money even though they know they're going to pay when you eventually die (which is a statistical certainty so far). In fact, the worst thing that could happen to the life insurance industry would be if we found a cure for mortality.

Because the death benefit in an IGIC is guaranteed, there are many more options than just payment at death. For example, a lot of life insurance policies will allow you to take out part of the death benefit *before you die.*

Because the death benefit in an IGIC is guaranteed, there are many more options than just payment at death. For example, a lot of life insurance policies will allow you to take out part of the death benefit before you die.

For example, if you are diagnosed as terminally ill, the IGIC may allow you to withdraw part of your death benefit while you are still alive. They know they are going to pay it when you die, so why not provide their insureds the money early and earn some major goodwill?

Additionally, if your doctor writes a letter certifying that you are no longer able to perform, without help, two of the six activities of daily living—eating, bathing, getting dressed, toileting, transferring, and continence—the insurance company will pay a portion of your death benefit to you so you can pay for the care that you need. It's almost like long-term care insurance, except it is a lot cheaper with far fewer restrictions. In fact, many insurers will include it without charging for an additional rider since they're going to be paying out on the death benefit anyway. They do that to gain a competitive advantage over other insurers.

The IGIC, like qualified plans, is asset protected,[29] though the degree of protection varies from state to state.[30] If you incur some sort of debt that results

---

29. *See, e.g., DC Mex Holdings LLC v. Affordable Land LLC,* 320 Mich. App. 528, 907 N.W.2d 611 (2017).
30. For a survey of the different states' laws, see "Can Your Cash Value Life Insurance Be Taken by Creditors?," Top Whole Life, last accessed May 18, 2020, https://topwholelife.com/can-your-cash value-life-insurance-be-taken-by-creditors.

in a judgment against you, your creditors may be able to garnish your wages, your bank account, or repossess your vehicle. However, subject to the particular exceptions in your state, your creditors cannot satisfy their judgment from the cash value of your life insurance or the death benefit.

CHAPTER 15

USING THE IGIC TO INVEST TAX FREE

"People who complain about taxes can be divided into two classes: men and women."

— Author unknown

WHY WOULD YOU EVER INVEST in anything taxed when you can invest in those same things tax free?

Those of you familiar with the Roth IRA will understand the power of tax-free growth.[1] You start with money you've already paid taxes on, invest it, let it grow, and no matter how much growth you experience, you'll never pay taxes again.

The problem with the Roth IRA is that the contribution limits are so low you could never retire on them, even if you maxed them out every working year of your life. Plus, if you make a decent living, you are disqualified from contributing.

The IGIC has many of the same benefits of the Roth IRA but without the limitations. That's why some call it the "Rich Man's Roth."

Let's look at a couple examples to illustrate the power of tax-free growth.

Let's say you have accumulated $100,000 in an IGIC. As your cash value grows, your death benefit does too. Let's say your death benefit at this point is $400,000. You decide you want to invest some of your money in real estate. You and your buddy find a home that you want to go in on together to do a fix and flip. The home costs $70,000, and you figure it will cost about $30,000 to fix it up.

You use the $100,000 cash value balance of your IGIC as collateral for $50,000 from the insurance company (your half of the total $100,000 to

---

1. For a review, read starting at page 69.

flip the house). The insurance company doesn't check your credit. You don't have to apply. You just tell them you want it (you don't even tell them why). A day or two later, the money is sitting in your checking account. Your loan is accruing simple interest at 5 percent annually. You are free to pay it back at your pace and on your terms, or if you want, you can choose not to repay it at all.[2]

Your buddy has $100,000 in his 401(k). After he finds out what you've done, he asks his broker if he can use his 401(k) money as collateral for a loan. Nope. The IRS will not allow that.[3] He discovers that he can "borrow" money from his 401(k), though. The fact that the IRS calls it borrowing makes the money feel less like it's his and more like it belongs to the government.

As he goes through the process, he realizes it is not just a loan in name—it's an actual loan: he has to apply for it, agree to a repayment plan, and agree to pay interest, all of which is deducted from his paycheck to ensure the money gets repaid.

You two purchase the house. For several months, you both spend your evenings and weekends working on it. As expected, you put about $30,000 into fixing it up.

You market it for sale, and before too long, an eager buyer snatches it up for $140,000. You and your buddy each put in an equal share, and you agreed to split the profits. Each of you finish the transaction with $70,000. The entire process takes a year from start to finish.

You take your share to the insurance company. You use $52,500 to repay the loan ($50,000 for principal and $2,500 for interest, which accrued for a year at 5 percent), and the other $17,500 in profit gets added to your IGIC principal.[4] This profit gets added to the growth of the account and is not taxable in the

---

2. If you don't repay it, your death benefit will repay it for you when you die.
3. "Retirement Plans FAQs Regarding Loans," IRS.gov, last updated May 15, 2020, last accessed July 9, 2020, https://www.irs.gov/retirement-plans/retirement-plans-faqs-regarding-loans.
4. This won't work with all insurance contracts. An IGIC is set up to allow a cushion of profits to be put into the plan without the insurance contract turning into a MEC.

year you realized it. In fact, if you do it right, you won't ever have to pay taxes on it at all.[5]

In the meantime, in the year you pulled out your loan, your principal was still $100,000. You didn't actually touch the principal, so it still grew as though you'd never taken it out.[6] If between the guaranteed interest rate and dividends, your growth is 5 percent, then in the year your money was out, your IGIC actually grew by $5,000 (plus any premium payments you made along the way and any interest growth on them). That means the net cost to borrow against your policy was negative—you were actually paid to borrow money—in the amount of $2,500. That's the power of policy loan arbitrage (the difference in the interest you are earning versus paying).

Your buddy takes his $70,000 and pays back his loan too. We'll suppose that his loan was also 5 percent, so to repay his 401(k), he has to put $52,500 back in. The other $17,500 becomes taxable income that he adds to his other income and then pays taxes on it at his ordinary income rate.[7] If he's in the 24 percent tax bracket, then $4,200 of his earnings is lost to taxes.

In the meantime, in the year he was borrowing money, his 401(k) only had $50,000 in it instead of $100,000. One of two things happened while his money was away: either the stock market grew, or it didn't.

If the stock market grew at its average rate, 5.42 percent, then your buddy lost out on $2,710 in investment earnings. This brings his net earnings from $17,500 down to $13,300 after taxes, and down again to $10,590 after taking

---

5. We'll get into the details of it later, but because IGIC growth is tax deferred, it only gets taxed if you withdraw it from the policy, and only then after your withdrawal exceeds the principal you've put in. But if you retire on policy loans instead of withdrawals, then you never withdraw the growth. You also never pay taxes on it.
6. Not all insurance companies treat this the same way. It's the difference between direct recognition loans (where you earn the full interest on dividends on the *net* balance of your cash value, and you earn a lower amount on the rest) and nondirect recognition loans (where you get paid full interest and dividends on your *entire* cash value balance, regardless of any loans).
7. If he had held on to the property just a little longer so the investment exceeded one year, then he would only owe long-term capital gains taxes instead of short-term capital gains, which are taxed as ordinary income.

into account the opportunity cost of doing the investment. The better the stock market did in that year, the higher his opportunity cost.

If the investment stock market experienced a decline, it would do the opposite. For example, if this investment was from May 8, 2019[8] to May 7, 2020,[9] the Dow Jones saw an 8.05 percent loss. If his 401(k) performed similarly,[10] then his $50,000 in principal would have lost $4,025 (along with losses associated with any other principal he contributed in that year). The good news is that if he had not borrowed 50 percent of his money to invest in himself, his losses would have been double that, and his side investment helped offset the losses in the 401(k).

Your money was working for you in two places. You may not have even noticed the stock market hit because you aren't checking the stocks every day. They don't affect the value of your investment, which you know is always growing.

In the final scenario, regardless of what the market did, not including any principal contributions (premium payments) in the meantime, your account went from being worth $100,000 to being worth $122,500—an increase of 22.5 percent.

Your buddy, who put up the same amount of money, same amount of sweat equity, same amount of time, same risk, and same returns with average market growth, took his account from being worth $100,000 to being worth $113,300, an increase of 13.3 percent.[11]

In a down market with losses of 8.05 percent, he would have taken his account from $100,000 to $109,275, an increase of 9.275 percent.

---

8. The Dow Jones closed at 25,965.09 on May 8, 2019.
9. The Dow Jones closed at 23,875.89 on May 7, 2020. These are not arbitrary dates nor are they carefully selected to show loss. This is the last year exactly from the time I am writing this section.
10. If anything, with fees, it probably did worse.
11. His 401(k) would still only be worth $100,000 from the transaction. The $13,300 in profit is going to be after-tax dollars that are sitting in his checking account that he can use however he wants.

Of course, your buddy could always have taken his $17,500 in profit, paid it as his annual contribution to his 401(k) and not paid the taxes on it. But then he'd just have to pay taxes on it later with whatever growth occurred between now and then and at whatever rate the government decides to tax it on.

You see that it's not about *what* you invest in, it's *how* you invest. Whatever your preferred investment, the risk is what it is. But when your money is growing independent of—and at the same time as—your investment, and you know your growth is tax free, then you're actually risking a lot less than the guy paying taxes because he has to perform better (a lot better) to achieve the same net result.

CHAPTER 16

USING THE IGIC TO GET
OUT OF PERSONAL DEBT

"A man in debt is so far a slave."
— Ralph Waldo Emerson

THESE DAYS IT IS HARD TO AVOID DEBT. We are taught about the importance of managing our finances but not taught what that really means or how to do it. The importance of getting an education is drilled into us since our childhood, but tuition continues to grow far faster than inflation[1] and about eight times faster than wages.[2] Materialism and consumerism are made ever-more attractive by targeted advertisements that track our locations, interests, and browser history[3] while access to stuff is increasingly easy. Every time you check the mail, one credit card or another is offering you a line of credit.

Just as prolific are experts, pundits, and gurus telling you how to get out of debt. Some are scams. The most effective of the experts tell you that you have to live on beans and rice, cut back on your lifestyle, and scrimp and save until several years later, you can call in to a radio show, proclaim financial freedom, and then hang up the phone. You then realize that although you're

1. Kaitlin Mulhere, "Here's How Much Colleges Are Actually Charging in 2019," money.com, November 6, 2019, last accessed July 9, 2020, https://money.com/heres-how-much-colleges-are-actually-charging-in-2019.
2. Camilo Maldonado, "Price of College Increasing Almost 8 Times Faster Than Wages," forbes.com, July 24, 2018, last accessed July 9, 2020, https://www.forbes.com/sites/camilomaldonado/2018/07/24/price-of-college-increasing-almost-8-times-faster-than-wages.
3. Hannah Middleton, "Geofencing & Geoframing: The What, Why, and How of Location Targeting," choozle.com, April 16, 2019, last accessed May 17, 2020, https://choozle.com/blog/geofencing-geoframing-location-targeting.

out of debt, you don't have anything saved for retirement. The only cash to your name is the emergency fund that will last you a few months if you were to lose your job. You don't have anything saved up because you fell for the conventional wisdom that tells you we can't pay off debt and set aside money for retirement at the same time. Because you can only use money once, you have to pick between the two.

You picked debt because it was more urgent. Retirement is years away, but your debt exists now. Besides, if you save for retirement instead, your debt will balloon and eventually ruin your retirement if it doesn't bankrupt you first.

That's where conventional wisdom has failed you again. It has placed you in shackles and made you believe that you can only use your money once. Your dollar can go to pay off debt, or it can go to save for retirement. Or to buy food. Or go to a movie.

Indeed, if your retirement plan consists of contributing to a 401(k), that's true. Because when you put money into a 401(k), it's not really yours anymore.[4] So you can't leverage it, borrow against it, or otherwise use it for anything else.

But we need to stop thinking so one dimensionally. Using the leveraging power of an IGIC, we can use our money to pay off debt, save for retirement, and as our rainy-day fund all at the same time (and for many other uses, which we'll discuss in subsequent chapters).

Using the leveraging power of an IGIC, we can use our money to pay off debt, save for retirement, and as our rainy-day fund all at the same time.

Let's use Sam and Max as examples.

---

4. *See* discussion about property rights starting at page 37.

Sam the Doctor with Student Loan Debt

Sam is a recently graduated doctor in her first year of practice.[5] She has worked hard to stay out of consumer debt but owes on a vehicle, student loans, and her mortgage:

	Interest	Debt	Payment
Car	4.90%	$30,246	$525
Student Loans	6.00%	$220,429	$2,000
Personal Residence	4.50%	$271,331	$1,383
Total Debt	**5.16%**	**$522,005**	**$3,908**

At the current rate of payment, Sam will pay off all of her debt in 29.7 years, with the last payment on her mortgage being made just a few months shy of thirty years from now. But she won't have just repaid $522,005:

- Total debt: $522,005
- Total interest paid: $325,575
- **Actual debt: $847,580**

That means on average every month, $913.51 is going to interest alone! That's really why debt is a growth-killer: interest.

Sam was lucky she came to see me right when she got out of medical school. She hadn't spent too much time paying down debt the old-fashioned way—you earn money, send it out the door toward debt, and you never see it again.

Instead, we drew up an IGIC. Sam would reduce her payments toward her debt to the minimum payments allowed. Then she would pay the difference, plus whatever else she was going to be contributing toward a 401(k) and

---

5. Sam was an actual client, but I have changed her name here to protect the identity of my client.

an emergency fund[6] into the IGIC. In her case, we drew up a plan for $5,000 monthly to go into the IGIC.

By putting the money first into the IGIC and then using it for debt, Sam can use that money more than once. It's growing for her at a guaranteed rate, plus she's earning nonguaranteed dividends. It is also paying off her debt, acting as an emergency fund, and providing a death benefit and living benefits.

As it grew, her debts would slowly (very slowly) shrink as she paid the minimum payments. But her IGIC was growing rather quickly. Then at a certain point, the balance of her smallest debt would be equivalent to 80 percent of the cash value in her account.

Once that happens, she was to borrow against 80 percent of the cash value and pay off the vehicle. Then she adds the monthly payment she was paying toward the vehicle to the $5,000 she's paying every month to the IGIC.

There is a very important reason we advise Sam not to borrow against more than 80 percent to pay off debt: We want to make sure she has an emergency fund to draw against to insure against life's unexpected expenses—hospital bills, fix a leaky roof, travel for a funeral, etc. Plus, we want to make sure the interest arbitrage (the difference between interest and dividends being earned on the total [the cash value] and interest accruing on the part [the loan]) is always positive so she actually makes money to take out a loan.

Sam can do the same thing with her other debts. She pays the minimum payment, continues to pay her premiums, and then when 80 percent of the cash value reaches the balance of the next-biggest debt (in her case, the student loans), she pays that off. Then she takes the monthly money she was paying toward the loan and rolls that into the total she contributes to her insurance contract.

When she does that, she can pay off the same debts, including her mortgage, in 7.1 years![7]

6. Because the IGIC is itself an emergency fund, there was no reason to continue to stick money into a savings account that wasn't any more liquid than an IGIC but was earning far less interest.
7. This program and the calculations presented here are made possible by Your Family Bank's proprietary debt-elimination software.

Remember, under the first scenario—the default scenario where she just continues to pay her debts—she is debt free in year 29.7, but she is also broke. In our scenario, in year 29.7—the year she would have been debt free under her conventional plan—she has $3,668,869 in retirement savings plus a $3,349,547 death benefit. Take a look at the side-by-side difference between the two:

	If Sam Had Kept Doing What She Was Doing	Using the IGIC
Debt Payoff	29.7 years	7.1 years
Interest Paid	$325,575	$131,352
Liquidity after 29.7 Years	$0	$3,668,869

Amazing, right? We're not all making doctor wages, though. So let's look at another actual client's example.[8]

Max the Accountant with Consumer Debt

Max is an accountant who has not been quite so careful to stay out of consumer debt. He has a few credit cards, a car loan, and a balance on his mortgage:

	Interest	Debt	Payment
Credit Card 1	19.90%	$4,000	$115
Credit Card 2	16.90%	$6,603	$170
Credit Card 3	18.70%	$10,587	$262
Car Loan	3.59%	$47,199	$779
Personal Residence	5.09%	$146,500	$805
Total Debt	**5.16%**	**$214,889**	**$2,131**

8. I have changed the name to protect my client's identity.

Again, that's not the end of the analysis because the total principal is different than the total debt, which includes interest. The amount of interest you pay depends on how long it takes you to pay it off. In Max's case, 29.1 years means paying another 70 percent on top of the principal he owes:

- Total debt: $214,889
- Total interest paid: $150,743
- **Actual debt: $365,632**

For Max, we were able to divert $1,300 per month toward the plan. Some of that came from credit card overpayments, some of it came from a term insurance premium,[9] and some came from money he was putting toward an emergency fund or 401(k).

By putting the money first into the IGIC and then using it for debt, Max can use that money more than once. It's growing for him at a guaranteed rate, is earning nonguaranteed dividends, and it is also paying off his debt, acting as an emergency fund, and providing a death benefit and living benefits.

In his scenario, he would be able to save $91,396 in interest, then use that savings so interest was working for him instead of against him. At the end of 29.1 years (the point when he would have been debt free but broke under the conventional scenario), he would have $1,272,417 in liquidity plus a $876,812 death benefit. Here are the two scenarios back to back:

---

9. Once the IGIC was set up, he had a growing death benefit and did not need term insurance anymore.

	If Max Had Kept Doing What He Was Doing	Using the IGIC
Debt Payoff	29.1 years	7.1 years
Interest Paid	$150,743	$59,347
Liquidity after 29.1 Years	$0	$1,272,417

The best part about these plans is that Sam and Max aren't really spending any more than they were already spending. They aren't scrimping and saving, living on rice and beans, and living a pauper's lifestyle. They are just diverting their money so that their money is working for them before they use it for debt. That way, their cash is always accumulating even as their debt is shrinking. So the power of interest is working in their favor.

The $1.27 million that Max has after 29.1 years is not going to be enough for retirement. He is definitely going to need to set up some other sort of retirement plan, perhaps another IGIC. But that's okay. Max knew that $1,300 monthly was never enough to build a good retirement. His purpose in diverting that money wasn't just to build part of a retirement. His main purpose was to pay off thirty years' worth of debt, which he was able to accomplish in 7.1 years.

But because Max now understands the power of having interest work in his favor, he's not going to be financing any future purchases through a bank. He's going to finance them through his insurance contract. And he's probably going to start a second IGIC. When it comes time to retire, Max will not only be debt free, but he'll have a healthy tax-free retirement fund.

CHAPTER 17

USING THE IGIC TO PAY FOR A CHILD'S TUITION

"An investment in knowledge pays the best interest."
—Benjamin Franklin

PARENTS CAN HELP THEIR CHILDREN plan for a successful future in a number of ways. Mine subscribed to the if-he-wants-to-go-to-college-he-can-pay-for-it plan. I probably would not have even gone to college myself except that my dad also put me to work doing hard labor for his construction company during my high school summer breaks. Those experiences convinced me that no matter what I did, I wanted to be paid for my brain and not my body. College seemed the best way to do that.

To pay for college in 2020, the average student is going to need $41,426 to go to a private school; $27,120 for a public school paying out-of-state tuition; and $11,260 for a public school paying in-state tuition.[1] That's just for one year. The student will have to pay it again their sophomore year. Those costs have risen dramatically over the last twenty years when those same respective averages at that time were $16,294; $9,639; and $3,508.

Traditionally, there are three ways to pay for school: paying cash, using a 529 savings plan, and taking out student loans. Each of them has significant drawbacks, and none of them hold a candle to using the IGIC.

---

1. Briana Boyington and Emma Kerr, "20 Years of Tuition Growth and National Universities," U.S. News and World Report, September 19, 2019, last accessed May 18, 2020, https://www.usnews.com/education/best-colleges/paying-for-college/articles/2017-09-20/see-20-years-of-tuition-growth-at-national-universities.

SAVING UP AND PAYING CASH

Conventional wisdom tells us that paying cash is the best and smartest way to make purchases and investments because going into debt is bad.

If you follow this approach, you'll start sticking money away while your child is young. It will sit in an account, grow at a rate that doesn't even match inflation, and then when it is time for your kids to go to college, you'll have them covered. Or maybe you'll stick money in a bond where it will be locked up until it matures just in time for you to cash it out and pay for schooling.

Either way, you are losing investment and growth opportunities—opportunities you don't want to take because you don't want to risk money for your child's education—while your money is only working for you once.

But the ultrawealthy understand that when you store cash, it isn't working for you, and when you pay cash, that money is gone and can never work for you again.

So paying cash isn't exactly a terrible plan—it's better than not planning at all—but it comes at the opportunity cost of whatever it would be worth if your money were working for you.

Moreover, when it comes time to go to college, if your kids want to qualify for need-based financial aid or grants, that cash sitting in *your* savings account (or in your wallet or under your mattress) counts against them and may disqualify them for the aid.[2]

Saving up for college using cash is not a terrible plan, but it is far from ideal.

---

2. Fastweb Team, "How Can One Shelter Parent Assets on the FAFSA?" Fastweb, September 14, 2017, last accessed July 9, 2020, https://www.fastweb.com/financial-aid/articles/how-can-one-shelter-parent-assets-on-the-fafsa.

THE 529 SAVINGS PLAN

The 529 savings plan is named after—you guessed it—section 529 of the tax code.[3] If you read Part I of the book, you probably don't have to read up any further on the 529. You know it's part of the government's tax collection plan, so it's not something you want to put your money in. And you're right. You probably don't need to know anything more than that.

A 529 plan allows you to contribute money into an account that can grow and later be used for school-related expenses. They are state administered, which means that they vary from state to state. You do not get a federal tax deduction for your contributions (some states will allow a deduction), but the allure of the plans is that you can then use the funds, including the growth, without paying taxes on them as long as they are for qualified educational expenses.

All told, there really are only two advantages to a 529 plan: (1) the growth on the principal is tax deferred and will be tax free when withdrawn for qualified educational expenses, and (2) some states offer a tax deduction on state income taxes for contributions.

But there are significant disadvantages. For one, you have limited investment options, much like with a 401(k). Usually, you're going to be investing in mutual funds, which comes with the same ups and downs as with your 401(k) investments.[4]

For another, once the money goes in, it can only come out within the narrow confines of the rules governing the plan. In the case of the 529 plan, like the 401(k), if you withdraw outside the confines of those plans, you'll pay a 10 percent penalty and taxes on anything you haven't already paid taxes on (the growth).

Maybe your child wants to enroll in a nontraditional education that does not qualify as an educational expense. Maybe your child wants to skip college and start a business. If that's true, then you're either going to have to reallocate

3. 26 U.S.C. § 529, to be precise.
4. *See* discussion starting on page 53.

that money to someone else for educational expenses (someone whose educa-tion you probably wouldn't have offered to pay for otherwise) or use the money elsewhere and take the penalty.

Or, you could find yourself in the situation of one of my paralegals. She used a 529 savings plan to get two degrees, and there were still tens of thousands of dollars left in the plan. Now she can either go get a third degree she doesn't need or want or withdraw it, pay the penalty, and take the tax hit. Or she could let the money go to her cousin to use for educational expenses.

Using your money to put someone else in a better position is great—I'm not trying to suggest otherwise. But that should be your choice, not something that is forced upon you by an overly restrictive tax-generation device.

The final problem with the 529 account is the same one as paying cash. The money in the account is going to be included when determining need and could potentially disqualify your child. You are effectively penalized for planning ahead.

STUDENT LOANS

This was my plan. During my undergraduate years, I was able to minimize my student loans by taking a semester off every year or two to work full time and save up for the next semester. But by the time I entered law school, I couldn't afford the part-time pace (and full time was a requirement at my school). I had a wife and a baby when I started law school, with another one on the way.[5]

Because I had no other plan or tuition savings, I relied on my merit-based scholarship to offset the cost of tuition and the student loans to cover part of tuition, all educational expenses and all living expenses for my entire family that weren't covered by my part-time pizza-delivery job.

When I graduated from law school, I had just over $150,000 in student loan debt.

---

5. Another baby, not another wife.

That didn't really bother me because I figured with my big lawyer salary, I could pay that off in no time. Reality set in a few years later when I had contributed about $90,000 to my student loan balance, but I still owed $135,000, having only paid off $15,000 in principal.[6]

Anyone who had to take out student loans to fund their education knows the burden of repaying them. It's like paying a second mortgage. Its due whether your education ends up serving you or not. And unless you can show undue hardship (a high burden), student loans are not dischargeable in bankruptcy.[7]

USING THE IGIC

Remember how the cash value of an IGIC can be used for any purpose?[8] One of those purposes is paying for college.

Let's say you're expecting a child, and you want to start saving ahead for college. You set up an IGIC where you put in $2,000 per year for the first eighteen years of their life.

Although your child is the insured, you're the owner of the policy, so you can use it just like you would any other IGIC. As the cash value grows, you can use it to invest, pay off debt, whatever you want. Instead of using your own cash or bank-financed money, you're financing it yourself, and you're paying yourself interest. You can grow money outside the policy even as it is growing inside the policy, just like any other IGIC.

When your child is eighteen, you will have put in $36,000. The internal growth on the insurance contract, including guaranteed premiums and projected dividends, will bring your total to $54,353. That doesn't include any benefits you would have gotten by using it in the meantime.

---

6. Incidentally, two years after starting my first IGIC, I was able to pay off the entirety of my student loans, which would have taken another eight or so years on my non-IGIC trajectory.
7. 11 U.S.C. 523(a)(8).
8. See discussion beginning on page 143.

If that were the end of the analysis, it is a good deal, but we're not quite in amazing territory yet. So consider the other benefits.

This cash value can be used toward anything (anything you, as the owner, approve). If your kids want to use it for tuition, they can. Books. Room and board. Purchase a vehicle. Start a business. The sky is the limit. Because they're not withdrawing the money but taking policy loans, their use of the funds is not taxed.[9]

The $54,353 is probably not going to be enough to pay for school alone, but that's okay. Your child can apply for financial aid and need- and merit-based grants. That cash value is not a reportable asset,[10] so it won't have any negative impact on their efforts at procuring aid.

We don't have to go any farther than that to see how much better this is for tuition than cash, a 529 plan, or student loans. But that's not it.

If you want your child to earn part of their own way, and you own your own business, you can put them to work. Any reasonable wages you pay them for their work (and wages can be contributed to the IGIC) are tax deductible (up to $12,200 per year as of 2020). In some circumstances, you don't have to pay employment taxes on their wages (unemployment, Social Security, and Medicare).

Let's assume that you choose to write up the insurance contract so that it is fully paid up at age eighteen. That means once you've put in your $36,000, you never have to make another premium payment. The cash value is guaranteed to continue to grow, and the death benefit is guaranteed to pay out.

Assume also that your child uses the money for school and pays back the money used (which they can do on their own terms and timeline). They do this for the purpose of maximizing the interest arbitrage on the policy. Then once they graduate college, you transfer ownership of the policy to them.

---

9. Even if they withdrew it instead of using policy loans, there would be no taxes on the first $36,000 withdrawn.
10. "Asset Net Worth," FAFSA, last accessed July 9, 2020, https://fafsa.ed.gov/help/assetnetworth.htm.

Without putting in any more premium but the $36,000, your child will have an account that continues to grow their entire life that they can access to invest, use as an emergency fund (or for anything, really), and ultimately use to supplement whatever other retirement they have built.

By the time your child turns sixty-five, that $36,000 will have turned into $826,927 in cash value propped up by a $1.6 million death benefit. At age seventy, the cash value will be $1.08 million and the death benefit $1.864 million. Both numbers continue to rise. If your child passes at age ninety, the cash value will have ballooned to $2.8 million, which means that is the total they could have leveraged over the life of their retirement. Their heirs will get a death benefit of $3.26 million, less any outstanding policy loans—completely tax free.

Remember, all of this was from a few payments made early in their life, was something you were able to use while they were kids, something that paid for their schooling, and does not include any contributions they made to their own retirement. How's that for a cool way to pay for school?

CHAPTER 18

USING THE IGIC TO FINANCE YOUR BUSINESS

"Whether you think you can, or think you can't—you're right."

– HENRY FORD

IF YOU'RE A BUSINESS OWNER, or thinking about becoming one, the IGIC could change the way you do business. In fact, it was this facet of the program that was first introduced to me.

Several years ago, I started a civil trial firm. We represented injured victims of other people's intentional and careless behaviors. Ne'er-do-wells attacking unsuspecting victims in parking garages. Doctors putting prosthetic parts in backwards. Casinos using chairs at their slot machines that had a history of collapsing beneath their patrons.

I didn't start the firm until I had several years' experience in civil litigation, so I understood the legal aspects of running a law firm. But what I didn't fully appreciate at the time was the extent of the costs that would be required to run a successful practice.

FINANCIAL PROFILE OF A SMALL TRIAL PRACTICE

You could use an IGIC to fund virtually any business, big or small. I'll show you how I used it at my practice and then explain how it could work with other business models.

One of the biggest initial hurdles of starting an injury law firm is the fact that money goes out the door every month even if money isn't coming in. Unless you're lucky enough to have a book full of clients the day you open your firm, money is not going to come in for a while. Between the overhead and the case costs, you are likely going to have to figure out how to survive for a time without taking any money home.

Even once you're established and money is flowing in both directions, that business-owner anxiety never completely goes away. As you grow, so does your overhead as you (1) expand offices (or move out of your in-laws' garage), (2) hire staff (or start paying your significant other, who was previously working for free), or (3) get a phone number that includes several of the same numbers in a row. (No self-respecting injury attorney has a phone number without repeating numbers, especially zeros.)[1]

If your employees are like mine, they want to get paid every time payday comes around, irrespective of how good that month has been. (It's so hard to find good help these days.) The landlord, the power company, the internet and phone companies—they all want to be paid and on time.

That, of course, is just another part of doing business, and it's not unique to our line of work.

The difference in what we were doing was in the case costs. Between filing documents, taking depositions, having exhibits made, and hiring experts, we could spend tens of thousands of dollars (and more) on a monthly basis just to move our cases forward. When you're not getting paid every month, that can be difficult.

All told, we could spend anywhere from $1,000 to $100,000 per case on these costs. As our firm grew, and we could afford to take on bigger cases, we found ourselves spending more money. Some large firms, like those taking mass tort cases, are spending tens of millions of dollars on their cases.[2]

---

1. Incidentally, mine is 702-550-7300.
2. Sara Randazzo and Jacob Bunge, "Inside the Mass-Tort Machine That Powers Thousands of Roundup Lawsuits," Wall Street Journal, November 25, 2019, last accessed July 9, 2020, https://www.wsj.com/articles/inside-the-mass-tort-machine-that-powers-thousands-of-roundup-lawsuits-11574700480.

These costs came out of our operating account—we were using our own money. That is part of the appeal for a client to hiring a trial law firm: they don't have to pay anything. Of course, there has to be money in the operating account if you're going to finance a case.

If you don't have your own money, a myriad of financing options exists for a personal injury law firm. Small business loans, financing specifically meant for injury firms, and fee-splitting with a firm who teams up with you and splits the costs are all options for making it possible to finance a case when you don't have enough in the coffers. Each of these options has its own benefits and drawbacks, which are probably fairly obvious and in any case beyond the scope of this chapter.

My firm was blessed not to ever have to borrow money to finance a case. We always paid the case costs with our own money. But that option also has significant downsides. When you put thousands of dollars into a case, and then you get repaid when the case comes to a conclusion a year or two later (maybe), you have, in effect, given your client an interest-free loan. Not only that, but you've missed out on the earning potential of using that money elsewhere.[3]

If we were able to successfully resolve the case, either through settlement, judgment, or verdict, we would be reimbursed for our costs. But that took months or years.

We figured there had to be a better way.

That's when my partner stumbled upon the IGIC. Neither of us had ever heard of it. We had the good stroke of luck to have a savvy life insurance agent in our networks. We learned a better way to run our law firm.

---

3. Granted, we were investing in the case, so it's not like the money was wasted.

HOW I USED AN IGIC
TO FINANCE MY LAW FIRM

When you know nothing of life insurance but what you see on commercials or hear on the radio, it would probably seem funny, maybe even absurd, to use life insurance to finance a trial firm's case costs. But now that you know how cash value insurance actually works, can you start to envision how it might be used to finance a business?

Remember, two aspects of cash value insurance contracts differentiate them from term policies. First, cash value insurance comes with a cash value (and therefore has much higher premiums for the same amount of death benefit), and second, cash value insurance contracts last until the insured dies (as long as the premiums are paid). This means the payout of the death benefit is almost guaranteed. It's like renting (term) versus buying (whole life) a house. In the short term, renting is cheaper, but when you buy, you're building equity, so you're typically better off in the long run.

An IGIC allows you to use the cash value of a whole life insurance account instead of taking out a loan from a bank. With the IGIC, you can borrow money from the insurance company using your cash account as collateral. You're borrowing against your contract instead of from it, so you never break the compound interest curve (i.e., the interest you earn always exceeds the interest you pay).

This concept capitalizes on the idea that if you buy with credit, you pay interest, and if you buy with cash, you lose interest. But if you're the bank, you get the best of both worlds.

So how does that work with a business? Well, we learned it was pretty simple.

First, we decided how much premium we were going to pay. We were a little tentative about the whole thing because committing to paying premiums for the forseeable future was intimidating. We ultimately decided that we would start with an insurance contract where we would pay $2,500 for each partner every month. We set it up so the premiums were "paid up" at retirement age, so no more premiums would be due. Additionally, it was set up so at any point in the future we could choose to lower the premiums to $1,000 monthly.

We set up our insurance contract differently than other whole life contracts. A typical whole life contract is set up for a death benefit. But to use it for firm financing and retirement, the idea is to maximize the cash-value-to-death-benefit ratio. So the cash value is maximized and wrapped with the minimum amount of death benefit required to preserve the preferred status of a life insurance account.[4]

Once the life insurance contract was set up (which required medical history information and a physical examination), the cash value started growing with every premium payment.

We continued to pay the smaller day-to-day costs, like filing fees and deposition expenses, using law firm funds. But when we had to make a large payment, like to get a custom trial animation or to hire an expert, we contacted the lending arm of our life insurance company and told them we would like to take out a loan using the cash value of our contracts as collateral. They then direct-deposited the funds into our bank account within a few days, which we then used for our cases.

The loans we took out did incur interest. But the interest we were earning on the cash value of our account outpaced the interest we had to pay on the loan, so it was still a net gain.

When we got paid on the case, we then would pay back the loan with interest. In the meantime, the cash value of our account had been growing through the guaranteed minimum interest paid to us, plus dividends, plus amounts added through further premium payments.

We explained to our clients that in lieu of giving an interest-free loan, we would be financing the larger case costs that would be incurring a 5 percent annual interest rate that would be paid out of any recovery. They were always more than willing to sign an agreement to that effect.

---

4. *See* discussion on the MEC formula at page 140.

The real purpose of setting up this account was to leverage the cash value to finance case costs. Since it is a cash account, we could also use it as a line of credit for other business expenses if needed. So if we had a couple of bad months, we could use it to cover overhead, or we could also rely on it to pay other firm expenses, like computers, software, or expansion.

Ultimately, not only did this allow for case financing, but it created tax-free income in retirement while keeping cash protected from creditors, predators, and legislators.

After all that, this is still life insurance, so it did have a death benefit, which just felt like a bonus. Not all IGICs are the same, but just to give you an idea with mine that had a $2,500 monthly premium,[5] the initial death benefit was $978,725. This benefit increased with every premium paid. At the end of five years, it would be $1.28 million, and at the end of ten years, it will have increased to $1.61 million, and so on.

The beauty of the growth was that the longer we had the IGICs, the bigger they got and the more we would have to draw on. This meant we could either take bigger cases or more cases, or both, and we would always have enough money to finance them.

Furthermore, if I live exactly as long as government statistics tell me I will live, I will die at age seventy-eight. At that point, my firm would have paid $667,902 in premiums.[6] The cash value (less whatever I use for retirement and assuming dividends continue to pay out at the long-established rate) will be $1,879,744. My heirs will receive a death benefit of $2,658,746.

But remember, the dividends aren't guaranteed, though most insurance companies will do everything they can to pay dividends. In my case, the actual values *outperformed* the projected values.

---

5. I was 37 when I started the policy and was given a preferred, nontobacco rating.
6. Different insurance contracts can be set up in different ways. For example, you can set one up so premium payments are not required after a certain age. So if you plan on retiring at age 65, you can set it up so at age 65 you stop paying premiums, but your life insurance contract continues on until your death. You can change the retirement or "paid-up" age later, too. You're not locked in to the age you select when you start.

At the *beginning* of year four, I paid my annual premium all at once. At the end of that year, I was projected to have $107,557.00 in cash value and a $1,203,771.00 death benefit. But in actuality, at the end of *year three* before I could benefit from that entire year of interest, my cash value was $108,167.31 ($610.31 higher than projected for the next year), and my death benefit was $1,206,194.84 ($2,423.84 higher than projected for the next year). When was the last time you did business with someone who underpromised and overdelivered?

By using life insurance to finance case costs, the money can be used multiple times. So far, I've used it twice: once to put away for retirement (with a death benefit for heirs as a bonus) and once as collateral for a loan for case costs. Over the next few decades, I can continue to use it even while it grows—for whatever I want (it's my money, after all). The last time I use it will be during retirement.

What Happened When I Sold My Trial Practice?

We didn't get started with the IGIC at my firm until we had already established ourselves. Just over two years into the plan, and frankly, because of the plan, I decided I wanted to dedicate myself full time to helping people do the same thing I had done.

After an unexpected announcement to a very understanding partner, we made arrangements for my partner to purchase the law practice from me so I could dedicate my full-time efforts to my new endeavor.

But what happened to the IGIC that the law firm was financing? Because it was mine, it would follow me wherever I went. There were still some loans outstanding that my partner arranged to pay when we split, so when I started with my new venture, there were no outstanding loans belonging to the trial practice.

At that point, I had a cash account with some $60,000 in cash value and about a million-dollar death benefit. I had a few options: I could (1) keep paying the full premium and continue with the plan the way it was written, (2) reduce the monthly premium and continue with a smaller plan, or (3) I could call the insurance company, tell them I wanted my account to be paid up, and then just enjoy whatever growth it would experience without any additional premiums.

Because I was starting a new business and already had a mature and growing cash account, I had my new business take over where the previous one left off (option 1). My new law firm continued to pay the premiums, and my tax-free retirement account continues to grow. In the meantime, although I am not litigating and don't have case costs, I still have operational expenses, marketing, etc. I have a significant account I can use toward those expenses without having to get a line of credit, solicit investors, or find other expensive methods of increasing working capital.

USING AN IGIC TO FUND ANY OTHER BUSINESS

It really doesn't matter what kind of business you own—whether you're a dentist with a small practice, or if you own an Etsy shop, a plumbing company, or a large corporation.

Examples abound of famous entrepreneurs who were able to start their company using cash value in life insurance. You don't have to look very far on the internet to find them: Ray Kroc (McDonald's), Walt Disney (Disneyland), Doris Christopher (Pampered Chef), and James Cash Penney (JC Penney), to name a few. There are undoubtedly countless others whose stories are less famous.[7] You could add my name to that list (the Fortune Law Firm).[8]

So how would it work for a small business owner? Let's take Sally the plumber, for example.

---

7. Since by their very nature, privately owned businesses are not public, and the origins of most businesses are not broadly publicized.
8. Fortune Law Firm, 11920 Southern Highlands Parkway, Suite 200, Las Vegas, Nevada 89141, 833-400-4999, contactus@fortunefirm.com, https://fortunefirm.com.

Sally owns a plumbing business that services homes throughout her metropolitan county. Her business does well in the day-to-day but sees fluctuating problems with debt, cash flow, taxes, and flexibility.

Running a business is expensive, and Sally's is no exception. She has the following business-related debts:

Debt	Interest Rate	Balance	Payment
Equipment	5.00%	$68,000	$4,000
Fleet of Trucks	4.25%	$130,000	$6,000
Construction Loan	4.50%	$1,250,000	$6,000
Line of Credit	5.99%	$40,000	$3,000
Materials	5.00%	$112,300	$5,000
Total Debt	**4.03%**	**$1,600,300**	**$24,000**

Sally is actually paying $12,675.53 over the minimum payments every month in hopes of paying off the debt sooner. Even so, at this rate, it will be 36.4 years until she pays off all of these debts. In the meantime, she will pay over $1,348,099 in interest! That's $3,086.31 going to debt every month!

Total debt: $1,600,300

Total interest paid: $1,248,099

Actual debt: $2,948,399

What's more is that at the end of 36.4 years, Sally is debt free, but she has no money sitting in her account—all her extra money has gone to debt.

What does this same scenario look like if the business owner pays into the IGIC first and then uses its cash leverage to pay off the debts so the money is working for her more than just once?

	If Sally Keeps Doing What She's Doing	If Sally Uses the IGIC[9]
Debt Payoff	28.6 years	8.0 years
Interest Paid	$1,348,099	$451,853
Sally's Liquidity after 36.4 Years	$0	$11,495,639

Just like using the IGIC to pay off personal debt, you can use it in your business. But since the scale of your business expenses is bigger than your personal expenses, the benefits of using the IGIC are much more dramatic.

---

9. These figures were calculated through Your Family Bank's proprietary debt-elimination software.

CHAPTER 19

CONVERTING A 401(K) OR OTHER QUALIFIED PLAN TO AN IGIC

"No taxes can be devised which are not more or less inconvenient and unpleasant."

– GEORGE WASHINGTON

BY NOW, if you've been persuaded at all by the words in this book, you're either regretting ever having put money in a 401(k) or relieved that you never did. If you have been regularly contributing to a qualified account, I have good news for you: playing by the government's rules, you can recharacterize that qualified money and stop the tax growth without any penalty or taxable event.[1]

Let's review your agreement with the government as it pertains to your qualified money.[2] Then let's discuss what options you have to start using for your benefit instead of everyone else's.

When you contribute to your 401(k), the government agrees not to tax you on that money in the year you contribute. In exchange, you promise you will follow whatever rules the government sets for your money for as long as it is in the 401(k). Some of those rules apply on the day you contribute. You understand that these rules are subject to change without notice or opportunity to renegotiate the terms, which include (1) paying a 10 percent penalty on anything withdrawn before age 59½, (2) withdrawing (and paying taxes on) an amount at least equal to your RMD (required minimum distributions) when you turn 72, (3) not using your money for what the government calls prohibited transactions, and (4) paying taxes on anything you ever withdraw at the then-current tax rate.

---

1. You will, of course, eventually have to pay taxes on the money you put in, but there is no taxable event in the rollover itself.
2. See discussion beginning at page 15.

There are a lot of rules about what you can and can't do with your qualified money. Fortunately, amidst the chaos of legislative strokes, there are some options, if only you know where to look.

Let's use Jack as an example. Jack started contributing to his 401(k) when he was thirty years old. In addition to what he contributed, his employer also did a partial max, up to a cap. After fifteen years of regular contributions and growth, Jack has $300,000 in his 401(k).

That's when Jack's parents retired. They had been regular contributors to a 401(k) for their entire working lives. They were led to believe that they were doing the right thing, but they started paying state and federal taxes on their 401(k) income and 85 percent of their Social Security income. Also, most of their deductions have expired. They don't have near the lifestyle they thought they earned after decades of retirement savings.

When Jack hears this, he is alarmed. He stops contributing to his 401(k) and begins to look for alternative investment vehicles. He understood there would be other places to put his money, but he is surprised to learn that he also has options for the $300,000 in his 401(k) that won't trigger any penalties or tax consequences.

That alternative is the IGIC. But Jack cannot simply take the balance of a 401(k) and use it to purchase an insurance contract. Remember, he has to play by the government's rules.

Jack realizes that his investment broker is handling his money and making money off of his money. He wants to be in the same position they are. He wants to be able to manage his own fund and determine what the fund should be used for.

So here's what Jack can do.[3] First, he moves the assets in the 401(k) from his brokerage account into a qualified structured account. He is going to get some pushback from his broker because the broker does not want to lose $300,000 from the assets she has under management. The broker may tell him

---

3. This is not something Jack can do on his own. He will need someone who understands tax law, structures, and has a life insurance license.

it's a terrible idea. She may even tell Jack it can't be done. But Jack knows better, and Jack is insistent, so the broker relents.

Every transfer Jack makes is going to be an assets-in-kind or like-kind transfer, so there is no penalty or tax consequence.

Now that Jack, and not his broker, has control of the money, he can create his own fund, a family fund—like a family office—where he can choose for himself the investments he would like his money to go into.

From here, Jack creates a special entity to manage his fund. This is no different than the funds you see on TV or in the newspaper or that perhaps you even participate in yourself. Jack also needs a second entity to find investments for the fund. If he doesn't already have one, he can set one up.

When he sets up the special LLC for the fund, he has to set it up with all the same rules as any other fund, which means he has to create a special operating agreement, subscription agreement, tax ID, tax election, and all the other internal governances and documents. This is necessary so the fund can be both IRS approved and specific to Jack.

Once he has all this set up, Jack understands that the fund has to have capital in it. Without capital, there is nothing to invest. Jack creates a share number and par value for the LLC. In Jack's case, he creates 300,000 membership units valued at one dollar each. Then he creates a direction of investment for the purchase of the membership units and transfers money from the structured account to capitalize the new LLC fund.

At this point, Jack has a fund and is free to invest his money how he wants—subject to rules against prohibited transactions. Although the growth is still going to be taxed at this juncture, Jack has more tax options now because he's running a business. That's when Jack looks around and realizes that if something were to happen to him—if he were to get hit by a car walking across the street—there would be nobody to run the fund. So Jack decides to get a key person insurance policy to ensure the perpetuity of the fund and allow it to continue long after he is gone.

That's when Jack goes to an insurance agent.[4] That insurance agent is going to collect some information about Jack—his date of birth, his annual income, his general health, and how much money he has and where it is invested. The insurance agent is going to be working within parameters set by his state's insurance commissioner and the IRS.

Those rules will not allow Jack to put the entire $300,000 into an insurance contract in one year. Plus, if he does, it will become a modified endowment contract, or MEC, which is subject to tax, and would obviate the purpose of Jack's strategy. Instead, they allow Jack to put in $100,000 each year for three years.

So that's how the insurance contract is written. Jack started off with $300,000 in his newly formed fund in the special LLC. At the beginning of the first year, he puts $100,000 into the insurance contract. He has, in essence, taken $100,000 from his right pocket and put it in his left pocket. Now he has $200,000 in his right pocket and $100,000 in his left pocket.

During the first year, he can take the $200,000 in the fund and pair it with the $100,000 in the insurance contract to invest.[5] When he does so, he is acting as a fiduciary and can pick and choose what he wants to invest in. The $200,000 in the fund is still subject to prohibited transactions, and growth is taxed, but the cash value in the insurance contract can be invested in anything, and growth is tax free.

At the beginning of year two, Jack is going to take another $100,000 from his right pocket, the fund, and put it in his left pocket, the insurance contract. Now he has $200,000 in his insurance contract and $100,000 in his fund. Once again, he can pair the money to invest.

After two years, at the beginning of year three, Jack takes the last $100,000 in his fund and puts it in his insurance contract. At this point, he has $300,000 in his insurance contract that he can use to invest.

---

4. Not just any insurance agent—it has to be one who understands tax law and structures or is affiliated with an entity that does. Most insurance agents won't touch a qualified account.
5. The cash value in year one will be less than $100,000 total because part of that sum will go to pay the insurance company's costs (including agent commissions) and the cost of the death benefit.

Now Jack is in a very, very good position.

Before Jack created this program, if he were to have bought stock on the stock market, held it until it grew, and then sold it, he would have to pay either long- or short-term capital gains, depending on how long he held it. If he were to have purchased real estate and sold it at a profit, he would have had to pay long- or short-term capital gains. If he were to have invested through his 401k, he would have only delayed his tax bill by snowballing his tax debt (i.e. tax deferrals). But instead of paying capital gains, he would have had to pay income tax when he retired—on the entire amount invested and all the growth.

But because Jack is now acting as a fiduciary on behalf of his insurance contract, the growth and profits are always 100 percent tax free.

But what about when Jack retires? What about required minimum distributions? Remember, that $300,000 is subject to Jack's deal with the government. Uncle Sam agreed not to tax him on the contributions. In exchange, among other things, Jack promised Uncle Sam that he would begin making withdrawals and paying taxes on them, no later than age seventy-two.

Jack still has to honor his agreement with Uncle Sam, but now, instead of being subject to RMDs and paying taxes on his whole retirement account, he only has to do that on the $300,000. He still has to pay taxes on the principal and growth for those fifteen years the money was in his 401(k), but he has effectively stopped the tax growth.

Let's assume that after Jack transfers his money into the insurance contract, he has fifteen years to invest it. It grows to one million dollars by the time his RMDs become due. He now has to pull out his RMDs on the $300,000 every year and pay taxes on it. His RMD that first year is going to be 3.9 percent,[6] or $11,718.75. Under current tax brackets, his taxes due (assuming no

---

6. We keep having to assume no changes in the tax code, but unfortunately there is no way to predict what Congress will do to make up their budget shortfall while selling the tax changes as something good for us. This calculation is made from the current RMD tax tables: "IRA Required Minimum Distribution Worksheet," IRS, last accessed May 21, 2020, https://www. irs.gov/pub/irs-tege/uniform_rmd_wksht.pdf.

deductions) would be $1,208.75. However, that's below the standard deduction for a nonitemized tax return,[7] which means Jack can honor his agreement with the government and still not have to pay any taxes.

Even if Congress were to do away with the standard deduction, and Jack did owe $1,208.75 in taxes, the one million dollars in his account is growing (not counting outside investments) by around $50,000 per year. The growth on the whole is more than enough to pay the taxes on the part. Plus, $1,208.75? If only. That's awesome. And $11,718.75 in taxable income is not enough to push Jack into taxation-on-Social-Security territory, so he gets to keep 100 percent of his Social Security income.[8]

Consider the alternative: Let's assume Jack leaves his $300,000 in his 401(k), and he continues to contribute like he always did. We will also assume that despite market fluctuations and corrections, when he retires, he has one million dollars in his 401(k). His required minimum distributions are going to be $39,062.50. That's not a very good retirement income (but then again, one million dollars is not enough to fund a good retirement). At today's tax rates, though, it's still something that taxes will reduce by $4,490 (not including deductions). Plus, as low as it is, it's still enough that Jack is going to have to pay taxes on 85 percent of his Social Security income.

How is all this possible? Under sections 101 and 7702 of the tax code, insurance contracts don't pay taxes. And that's been true longer than the tax code has been around.

Under sections 101 and 7702 of the tax code, insurance contracts don't pay taxes.

---

7. The standard nonitemized deduction in 2020 is $12,200 per person.
8. Depending on the amount of Social Security he qualifies for, the Social Security income itself may push Jack up into taxable territory.

CHAPTER 20

THE IGIC DURING RETIREMENT

"Anyone may arrange his affairs so that his taxes shall be as low
as possible; he is not bound to choose that pattern which best
pays the treasury. There is not even a patriotic duty
to increase one's taxes."

– JUDGE LEARNED HAND

RETIREMENT IS ONE OF THOSE THINGS that is really important—it may be the longest single source of a paycheck in your life—but it never seems very urgent while you are still working.

During the worldwide COVID-19 lockdown, we grew to appreciate the value of a regular paycheck more than any other time in this generation. Yet how concerned are we about our future paycheck—the one we'll cash during retirement when money is harder to come by because we're not working?

The problem with most retirement planning is just that—it is *only* retirement planning. Granted, retirement planning is not sexy. If you do it the conventional way, you are locking money away so your far-future self can use it. And it's hard to spend money on something without seeing the immediate benefit.

That's part of what makes the IGIC so amazing. You aren't just sticking money in a time capsule, burying it, only to open it thirty years later. You are planting a cherry tree that will not only feed you thirty years from now, but starting now, will provide cherries, shade, and beautiful perennial blossoms. You are sticking money somewhere that it will be guaranteed to grow. You'll still be able to use it whenever and for whatever you want, and you'll always know that money is yours. It's not earmarked for taxes. It isn't something creditors are going to take from you. It's yours.

Although the IGIC is something you can use and appreciate now, almost as a bonus, it has phenomenal value during retirement. Perhaps the easiest way to demonstrate it is to compare an IGIC retiree to someone who funded a government plan their whole lives.

So let's refer back to the example of the dentist in Chapter 5.[1] In that hypothetical, our dentist started her 401(k) plan as a thirty-one-year-old making $250,000 per year. She contributed $36,000 per year toward retirement ($19,500 in a 401[k] and $16,500 in a day-trading account). She did this consistently every year, paying her taxes as they became due, and taking her tax deductions on the 401(k) contributions. She planned to continue on this path until the age of sixty-five.

We ran several scenarios, taking into account a flat investment growth of 5.42 percent and no investment fees. In one scenario, instead of flat growth, we assumed fluctuating growth and loss with an average growth of 5.42 percent. Then we ran both scenarios with an average of 2 percent investment fees. We also ran a scenario where she got a $6,000 annual employer match. Under every scenario, we assumed that taxes would stay the same. We also did not account for state taxes.

Here are the best- and worst-case scenarios of our example:

	Scenario A Employer Matching	Scenario A Fluctuating Rates Average 5.42% with 2% Annual Fees
Total Invested at 65	$1,470,000.00	$1,260,000.00
Total Growth at 65	$2,629,014.60	$122,113.03
Total Accumulated at 65	$4,099,014.60	$1,382,113.03
Total Taxes Paid in Retirement	$1,408,696.54	$164,214.94
Years Before Money Runs Out	16.9	7.15

---

1. See example starting on page 48.

Let's create another scenario now—one in which a dentist contributes the same amount of money but uses an IGIC as the tax wrapper instead of the 401(k). We'll call this dentist Dr. B.

Dr. B earns the same amount of money as Dr. A and also starts contributing $3,000 per month to a retirement account on her thirty-first birthday. Instead of sticking her money into a 401(k) tax wrapper, Dr. B pays her taxes now and sticks her after-tax money into an investment grade insurance contract. On her thirty-first birthday, Dr. B knows exactly how her contract will perform because the terms are written in the contract. The insurance company guarantees a minimum growth and projects actual growth based on their historical dividend rate.

In fact, before she even agrees to contribute at all, the insurance company illustrates the performance of the IGIC over time in a year-by-year chart, which Dr. B can review before making a decision. In Dr. B's case, the chart, or illustration, looked like this:[2]

Year	Age	Contribution	Dividend	Cash Value	Death Benefit
1	31	$36,000.00	$458.00	$29,251.00	$1,710,437.00
2	32	$36,000.00	$1,020.00	$61,737.00	$1,893,354.00
3	33	$36,000.00	$2,077.00	$97,241.00	$2,073,623.00
4	34	$36,000.00	$3,312.00	$138,334.00	$2,251,145.00
5	35	$36,000.00	$4,318.00	$182,570.00	$2,426,254.00
6	36	$36,000.00	$5,469.00	$228,410.00	$2,599,959.00
7	37	$36,000.00	$6,727.00	$276,901.00	$2,772,831.00
8	38	$36,000.00	$8,068.00	$328,258.00	$2,945,274.00
9	39	$36,000.00	$9,519.00	$382,678.00	$3,117,662.00

2. This is an actual illustration run by a mutual insurance company using the parameters established in the hypothetical.

Year	Age	Contribution	Dividend	Cash Value	Death Benefit
10	40	$36,000.00	$10,947.00	$440,399.00	$3,290,216.00
11	41	$36,000.00	$12,480.00	$501,448.00	$3,462,931.00
12	42	$36,000.00	$14,163.00	$566,240.00	$3,636,044.00
13	43	$36,000.00	$15,982.00	$634,983.00	$3,809,908.00
14	44	$36,000.00	$17,850.00	$707,898.00	$3,984,725.00
15	45	$36,000.00	$19,885.00	$785,300.00	$4,160,584.00
16	46	$36,000.00	$21,863.00	$866,866.00	$4,337,606.00
17	47	$36,000.00	$24,044.00	$953,422.00	$4,515,611.00
18	48	$36,000.00	$26,342.00	$1,045,336.00	$4,694,916.00
19	49	$36,000.00	$28,877.00	$1,142,986.00	$4,875,708.00
20	50	$36,000.00	$31,455.00	$1,246,596.00	$5,058,204.00
21	51	$36,000.00	$34,195.00	$1,356,487.00	$5,242,359.00
22	52	$36,000.00	$36,917.00	$1,472,642.00	$5,428,164.00
23	53	$36,000.00	$39,898.00	$1,595,406.00	$5,615,472.00
24	54	$36,000.00	$43,164.00	$1,725,136.00	$5,804,727.00
25	55	$36,000.00	$46,577.00	$1,862,201.00	$5,996,237.00
26	56	$36,000.00	$50,145.00	$2,007,039.00	$6,190,082.00
27	57	$36,000.00	$53,920.00	$2,160,238.00	$6,386,371.00
28	58	$36,000.00	$57,863.00	$2,322,352.00	$6,585,227.00
29	59	$36,000.00	$61,973.00	$2,493,864.00	$6,786,671.00
30	60	$36,000.00	$66,317.00	$2,675,218.00	$6,990,783.00
31	61	$36,000.00	$71,048.00	$2,866,905.00	$7,197,587.00
32	62	$36,000.00	$76,258.00	$3,069,299.00	$7,408,404.00

Year	Age	Contribution	Dividend	Cash Value	Death Benefit
33	63	$36,000.00	$81,782.00	$3,282,679.00	$7,622,851.00
34	64	$36,000.00	$87,708.00	$2,507,601.00	$7,841,500.00
35	65	$36,000.00	$94,052.00	$3,744,648.00	$8,064,729.00

Dr. B understands that the dividends are not guaranteed, but that this particular insurance company has been paying them at competitive rates for over 170 years in a row.

Notice also that Dr. B's death benefit on day one is about $1.7 million. As she contributes to her account and the cash value grows, the death benefit also grows. The IGIC is designed this way to maintain the cash-value-to-death-benefit ratio required by the IRS to maintain the tax-favored status of an insurance contract. By the time she retires, her death benefit is just over $8 million.

Dr. B decides to put her money in this tax wrapper instead of a government-sponsored tax wrapper.

She does this for thirty-five years until, on the day before her sixty-sixth birthday, she retires. Before we look at what her retirement looks like over time, let's review the assumptions these numbers are based on. First, we are going to assume that the dividends pay out as projected. We are also going to assume that Dr. B has only contributed to her IGIC and never used the money in it to invest outside the insurance contract.

We don't have to make any assumptions about the tax rate because it doesn't matter. Dr. B's scenario is tax independent, so no matter how high taxes go, her retirement is going to look the same.

When she retires, she will have contributed $1,260,000 in after-tax dollars. As you can see from her illustration, it has now grown to $3,744,648.00.

Dr. B, like Dr. A, decides she would like a monthly retirement income of about $23,000 to maintain her lifestyle. She is going to withdraw $276,463 annually from her account—up to her basis of $1,260,000 (that's not taxed again). Then once she has depleted her basis, she is going to take out policy loans against the rest of the cash value (that's not taxed either because it's a loan).[3]

Under this scenario, Dr. B can maintain that lifestyle for over twenty years before she runs out of IGIC income:[4]

Year	Age	Retirement Income	Dividend	Net Cash Value	Net Death Benefit
36	66	$276,463.00	$91,590.00	$3,667,955.00	$7,389,576.00
37	67	$276,463.00	$89,900.00	$3,585,666.00	$7,010,631.00
38	68	$276,463.00	$87,854.00	$3,497,624.00	$6,639,238.00
39	69	$276,463.00	$85,718.00	$3,403,598.00	$6,274,717.00
40	70	$276,463.00	$85,271.00	$3,302,605.00	$6,018,193.00
41	71	$276,463.00	$87,292.00	$3,193,335.00	$5,877,988.00
42	72	$276,463.00	$89,417.00	$3,074,895.00	$5,722,227.00
43	73	$276,463.00	$91,715.00	$2,946,300.00	$5,550,419.00
44	74	$276,463.00	$94,129.00	$2,806,524.00	$5,362,025.00
45	75	$276,463.00	$96,594.00	$2,654,498.00	$5,156,358.00
46	76	$276,463.00	$102,317.00	$2,492,439.00	$4,935,858.00
47	77	$276,463.00	$105,106.00	$2,316,541.00	$4,698,454.00
48	78	$276,463.00	$107,729.00	$2,125,638.00	$4,441,329.00
49	79	$276,463.00	$110,313.00	$1,918,615.00	$4,163,367.00
50	80	$276,463.00	$112,920.00	$1,694,089.00	$3,863,539.00
51	81	$276,463.00	$115,467.00	$1,450,382.00	$3,540,719.00

---

3. This is not the only way to fund a retirement and not necessarily the best way. She could also have never withdrawn her basis and funded her retirement on policy loans alone.
4. This is a continuation beyond age 65 of the same illustration used to show Dr. B's contribution years.

Year	Age	Retirement Income	Dividend	Net Cash Value	Net Death Benefit
52	82	$276,463.00	$118,259.00	$1,185,818.00	$3,194,012.00
53	83	$276,463.00	$120,907.00	$878,799.00	$2,822,199.00
54	84	$276,463.00	$123,801.00	$587,468.00	$2,424,254.00
55	85	$276,463.00	$126,620.00	$249,524.00	$1,998,908.00

Let's change one of those assumptions. Let's suppose that instead of just letting her money sit in the account unused, Dr. B decides to use her cash value as collateral for loans, and with those loans, she invests.

Perhaps she invests in the stock market. She doesn't just leave her money in there, though, and she doesn't invest through a brokerage firm. Instead, she sets up an online account and buys low and doesn't sell until the stocks go up. When she cashes out, she puts the growth into her IGIC.

Or maybe Dr. B's investment of choice is real estate. She purchases houses using a tax-savings technique where she can get up to a 65 or 70 percent tax deduction on the price of the home in the year she bought it.[5] If she does that, she can purchase appreciating, revenue-generating assets that allow her to realize a large, immediate tax deduction.

No matter what she does with her money outside the policy, as long as it's growing, her net worth is growing. If she is savvy, she'll do it in a way that the growth is tax free and may even save her taxes from her dental income along the way.

Let's take a look again at Dr. A and Dr. B side by side:

5. This is known as cost-segregation real estate.
6. Depending on whether the employer matches.

	Dr. A	Dr. B
Total Invested at 65	$1.26–1.47M[6]	$1.26M
Total Growth at 65	$122k–$2.6M	$2.48M
Total Accumulated at 65	$1.38M–4.1M	$3.74M
Total Taxes Paid in Retirement	$164k–1.4M	$0
Years before Money Runs Out	7.15–16.9	20.9

Even in the best-case scenario—where growth is constant with no fluctuations, there are no brokerage fees, taxes don't go up, Dr. A lives in a state with no state taxes, and the employer contributes $6,000 annually to retirement—Dr. A's retirement is still four years shorter than Dr. B's.

Although Dr. B's scenario did rely on some nonguaranteed assumptions—the dividends—considering the historical trend, payment of consistent competitive dividends is far more likely than not. It's certainly far more likely than our assumptions for Dr. A about brokerage fees, market fluctuations, and taxes.

But how is it that Dr. B's retirement lasts so much longer when she stops working with $3.74 million in her retirement account, and in Dr. A's best case, she has almost $400,000 more at $4.1 million?

There are two major reasons for that. For one, Dr. A has to withdraw more money to maintain the same lifestyle because she has to pay taxes every year and has very few deductions remaining to offset that. To live on $23,000 per month, Dr. A has to withdraw $28,750 monthly,[7] so her retirement is depleting more rapidly than Dr. B's.

The second is that with every withdrawal from her 401(k), Dr. A's principal shrinks, which means any growth she experiences is on a smaller number. But when Dr. B is funding her retirement through loans, her principal doesn't

---

7. See page 51.

shrink—it grows. She isn't withdrawing it; she's using it as collateral for a loan. So it continues to earn guaranteed interest and nonguaranteed dividends.

What about those growing policy loans? Doesn't Dr. B have to repay those? If this were a 401(k), she would. If it were a bank loan, she would. But remember, unlike Dr. A pretending that the 401(k) money is hers, the money in Dr. B's IGIC is *actually* hers. So Dr. B sets the terms. During retirement, Dr. B chooses not to repay them. She knows she doesn't have to because she knows exactly what her rights are with her money. They're in the terms of a contract that both parties are bound to. Dr. B knows that when she eventually dies, the death benefit, which is fully paid for and guaranteed, will repay her policy loans, plus any interest that has accrued, and the remainder will go to her heirs tax free.

How. Cool. Is. That?

Our comparison doesn't end here, though.

Remember that whether your Social Security gets taxed depends on your taxable income. If you meet the very low threshold, you will have to pay taxes on between 50 and 85 percent of your Social Security income.[8]

Because your IGIC retirement paycheck is not taxable income, you will never meet those low taxable-income thresholds. You can enjoy your lifestyle *and* keep 100 percent of your Social Security income.[9]

The same is true for your Medicaid Part B and D coverage. They're not going to unduly increase because your taxable income is zero. You're unshackled. And that's a wonderful place to be.

The Most Important Distinction

If you look at that last chart again, you'll see that even Dr. B's retirement runs out after 20.9 years, which could very well be insufficient because Dr. B could live past age eighty-five. Although having access to 100 percent of her Social

---

8. See discussion beginning on page 65.
9. Unless your Social Security income alone pushes you up into those thresholds.

Security will help stretch that out a little, that won't be enough and shouldn't be part of any well-thought retirement plan anyway.[10]

You have to remember that although the 401(k) is purportedly a retirement plan, the IGIC is not. It isn't an investment. It isn't a retirement plan. It's an investment vehicle.

You have to remember that although the 401(k) is purportedly a retirement plan, the IGIC is not. It isn't an investment. It isn't a retirement plan. It's an investment *vehicle*. One of the assumptions we made drawing this up was that Dr. B was not investing outside the plan (to keep it comparable to the 401[k], which you *can't* invest outside the plan). But Dr. B should have been using the money *inside* the IGIC for collateral for investments *outside* the IGIC. That's the difference between an investment and an investment vehicle. Remember, the IGIC is just the tax wrapper for your investments.

A truly robust retirement plan is going to have Dr. B using the IGIC as the foundation for her entire retirement plan. For example, she could use the cash value of the IGIC as collateral, purchase some rental properties, take the immediate deductions, and with rental payments she receives, repay the loan in the IGIC. There are tax advantages to that (tax-free growth), and at the same time, Dr. B is purchasing an appreciating asset that produces income.

If Dr. B does this consistently, when she retires, she'll not only have her IGIC balance she can draw from, but she will also have several income-producing homes that will supplement her other retirement sources.

In this way, Dr. B will *never* run out of retirement funds. Because she's done something Dr. A could not. She's leveraged her investment vehicle to make her money work for her in multiple places at the same time. She has unshackled herself from the chains of conventional wisdom. Now *that's* a wonderful place to be.

---

10. If you want to know why you shouldn't bet on any publicly run plan, refer back to page 43.

CHAPTER 21

EMPLOYERS USING THE IGIC AS A 401(K) ALTERNATIVE

"Employees who believe that management is concerned about them as a whole person—not just an employee—are more productive, more satisfied, more fulfilled. Satisfied employees mean satisfied customers, which leads to profitability."

– ANNE M. MULCAHY

WE DISCUSSED IN THE FIRST CHAPTER[1] how employers, who had been writing blank checks to their employees through defined-benefit pension plans, were eager to replace these expensive, open-ended plans with the much-cheaper 401(k)s.

Recall that the defined-benefit pension plans were choking the life out of these companies. Just recently, forty years after the 401(k) entered the scene, Sears finally breathed its dying breath, attributing its demise to the $300 million in annual pension obligations.[2] It's hard to be profitable when you start out $300 million behind every year. When Sears made these promises to its employees in the 50s, 60s, and 70s, it had no way to know that life expectancy would increase by about eleven years.[3] Or, put another way, it had no way to know that it would be adding about eleven years onto its annual pension payments.

This shift placed the burden of retirement on the employee rather than the employer. Those employers (and there were droves of them) who switched to the 401(k) thought little about the annual costs for maintaining these programs.

---

1. See discussion starting on page 12.
2. See page 13.
3. Max Roser, Esteban Ortiz-Ospina, and Hannah Ritchie, "Life Expectancy," Our World in Data, October 2019, last accessed June 5, 2020, https://ourworldindata.org/life-expectancy.

It felt nominal compared to the much higher pension obligations they had committed to in the past.

But the costs of implementing and maintaining a 401(k) program as an employer are hardly insignificant.

Even small businesses setting up small plans (with a total value of less than one million dollars) have to pay up to $3,000 to start a 401(k) program.[4] That cost, which doesn't include any of the regular and annual maintenance fees, is one many employers willingly bear to provide this retirement benefit and remain competitive with other employers.

The costs of maintaining a plan are even higher. Even small employers can pay over $10,000 annually to maintain these plans.[5] This includes administrative fees, monthly charges per employee, and compliance-related fees.[6] There can be thousands more in investment and consultant fees, too.

One of those compliance-related fees involves the annual testing that is mandatory for all 401(k) sponsors (employers). The IRS requires employers to treat all employees equally with the 401(k). They enforce this with annual testing,[7] and the employer has to pay for it.

The rule was created so employers could not contribute a disproportionate amount to their own 401(k) (or to high-salary or other favored employees) while contributing little or nothing at all to other qualifying employees.

Perhaps one reason employers are willing to pay all these fees for a 401(k) is that they aren't aware that defined-benefit pension plans and 401(k)s, though certainly the most well-known options for employer-sponsored retirement plans, are not the only options. They're not even the best options.

4. "How Much Does a 401(k) Cost Employers?," Human Interest, June 15, 2020, last accessed July 9, 2020, https://humaninterest.com/blog/how-much-does-a-401k-cost-employers.
5. Id.
6. Id.
7. "401(k) Plan Fix-It Guide—The Plan Failed the 401(k) ADP and ACP Nondiscrimination Tests," IRS.gov, last accessed June 5, 2020, https://www.irs.gov/retirement-plans/401k-plan-fix-it-guide-the-plan-failed-the-401k-adp-and-acp-nondiscrimination-tests.

Indeed, the IGIC can be used by any employer as a substitute. Not only is it better for the employee, but it is also better for the employer.

We have compared and discussed at length how the IGIC compares to the 401(k) from the plan owner's (in this case, the employee's) perspective.[8] But looking at the plan from the employer's perspective is just as compelling.

One of the biggest benefits of the IGIC for the employer is its flexibility. Because it is a private plan, not a government plan,[9] it is not bogged down by a labyrinth of bureaucratic hoops, limitations, and hidden costs.

If an employer wants to set up a retirement plan for its employees using an IGIC, it can do so on its own terms. It can set up as many or as few as it wants, for whatever employees it wants, in whatever amount it wants.[10] If the employer is helping its employees convert their qualified accounts to an IGIC, there are some modest governmental costs.[11] Otherwise, the cost to the employer for setting up an IGIC-based retirement plan is zero. Nor are there any maintenance fees.

As incredible as it may sound, if an employer wants to set up an employee retirement plan with an IGIC, there are no set-up or maintenance costs, and the employer will never have to pay any more than what it chooses to contribute to the plan.

Other benefits to the employer of this plan are its contributions that are 100 percent tax deductible.[12] It can choose to use the cash value of the employee plans for its business (like a growing cash account), and these plans breed employee loyalty and longevity.

---

8. Open up this book to any random page and you're bound to hit one that illustrates this point.
9. See discussion beginning on page 43.
10. The employer would obviously have to stay within the insurability limits of the insurance company. But there are so many options for maximizing or multiplying cash value that this seldom becomes an issue, and even then, only after far more is contributed than would fit in a qualified plan.
11. See discussion beginning on page 189.
12. Mark P. Cussen, "Insurance-Based Tax Deductions You May Be Missing," Investopedia, January 19, 2020, last accessed July 9, 2020, https://www.investopedia.com/articles/tax/09/personal-business-tax-tips.asp.

Let's use a few examples to illustrate the powerful advantages of this 401(k) alternative.

Small Business Owner Setting Up A Retirement Plan for Its Employees

Roy Parker owns a heating and plumbing business called "Big Roy's Heating and Plumbing."[13] He started his business working on his own but was quickly busy enough to need a receptionist, dispatcher, and a team of plumbers. He has six employees and would really like to reward them so that they see this as more of a career than a job. He doesn't want them to ever consider working anywhere else.

Roy puts a lot of effort into promoting a hard-working but fun atmosphere, but he knows that retirement is important to his employees, knows that some other plumbing employers in the area do 401(k) matches, and believes his employees will really appreciate the gesture. Plus, with all the money he spent getting this business up and running, he hasn't really been contributing to his own retirement account and wants to start.

Roy is familiar with the 401(k) and assumes that's what he wants to do. (This book hadn't come out when Roy was at this crossroads.) He looks into it and learns that in his case, it will cost $1,750 to set up a 401(k), $850 in administrative fees, and $25 per employee per month. If he sets one up for himself and his employees, that is $4,700 in the first year. That doesn't count any of the money he would contribute to the actual fund.

Then he finds out he'll have to pay for investment advice and consulting fees, nondiscrimination testing fees, and other miscellaneous fees. His broker says, only after Roy did independent research and asked about the fees, that these amounts are "hard to calculate and are assessed on a case-by-case basis."

Roy is discouraged, especially when he realizes it probably won't breed much employee loyalty. His broker is telling him it will, but if other plumbing

---

13. These names, as well as those in the other examples in this chapter, are fictitious names.

operations are also offering 401(k)s, and an employee can take their 401(k) from one job to another, then there is no added incentive to stay with him.

He's not sure it is worth it.

That's when he finds out about the IGIC, which changes his and his employees' trajectories forever.

Roy has a part-time secretary/bookkeeper, full-time dispatcher, and four full-time plumbers. One of the plumbers has been with him a long time and is a foreman. He's an invaluable part of the team.

Roy creates an amazing program:

1. Roy sets up an IGIC for himself. He contributes $5,000 per month. It has an immediate death benefit of $2.1 million. After twenty-five years, between the guaranteed interest and nonguaranteed dividends, the cash account is projected to have grown to $2.48 million and the death benefit to just over $6 million.

2. Roy sets up an IGIC for his foreman. He contributes $1,000 per month. It has an immediate death benefit of $450,000. After thirty years (the foreman is younger than Roy), the cash account is projected to have grown to $768,181 with a death benefit of $1,735,422. The cash account is in the foreman's name, and the foreman chooses his wife to be the beneficiary of the death benefit.

3. Roy sets up four more separate IGIC accounts for his three other plumbers and his dispatcher. For each of them, he reaches an agreement that he will contribute $500 per month, and the employees will each contribute $500 per month into their individual accounts. For every year they work with him, on the anniversary of their hire date, he will increase his contribution by one hundred dollars per month, and the employee's share will shrink by one hundred dollars per month. So by the end of five years, he will be contributing the full $1,000 monthly to their accounts. They each pick the beneficiary of the death benefit.

Their cash value and death benefit numbers are similar to the foreman's, but they have to contribute more to their funds at the beginning.

4. Roy tells the secretary that when she reaches her one-year anniversary with the company, or if she starts working full time, whichever one comes first, he will set up a policy for her.

In the first year of the plan, Roy pays exactly $96,000 toward these plans ($60,000 toward his and $36,000 toward his employees). He is pleased to discover that not only were there no hidden costs, he didn't have to come up with any additional money at all to set up or maintain these plans. The contributions are tax deductible to the business as employee compensation.

However, this counts as income to the employees, so the employees (including Roy) must pay tax on it as income in the year the contributions were made. The employees actually prefer it this way, though, because they don't fall for the follies of conventional "wisdom." They understand they are better off paying taxes now at a known rate and enjoying tax-free growth than paying taxes later at an unknowable (and probably higher) rate on the contributions and the growth.

The employees now have an account that is growing every time a premium is paid, interest accrues, or a dividend is paid. And it is liquid. There are no penalties if they want to access it, so they can use it to invest, pay off debt, and use it just like any other IGIC. The money will keep growing while it's inside the policy. Plus, if the unthinkable should happen and mortality strikes, their family will be taken care of.

One of the plumbers gets a job offer from a competing plumbing company. That plumbing company is offering to pay $3,000 more per year than he is getting from Roy. It is also willing to offer the industry-standard 50 percent match up to 6 percent of the total income to a 401(k) plan. Since the plumber would make $53,000, to maximize the match, he would have to contribute $530 per month ($6,360 per year). The employer would contribute $265 per month ($530 x 0.50 = $265 x 12 months = $3,180 per year). Total contributions per year would be $9,540 ($6,360 + $3,180).

The plumber right now is earning $50,000 in wages, contributes $500 per month ($6,000 per year), which is exactly what Roy is contributing, bringing his total contribution to $1,000 per month ($12,000 per year). He knows that if he leaves his job, the IGIC is his, but Roy will no longer contribute to it. He will either have to surrender the policy (take the cash value and lose the death benefit), change it to reduce the premiums to $500 monthly (and cut his death benefit and potential cash value in half), or come up with the extra $6,000 per year to keep it live.

Plus, after having had the IGIC for a year, he can't imagine wanting to put money into a 401(k). Now that he has seen it for what it is, he can't unsee it. As tempting as that extra wage would be, when he does the math, it just doesn't support the move.

After having had the IGIC for a year, he can't imagine wanting to put money into a 401(k). Now that he has seen it for what it is, he can't unsee it.

Roy has created a program that he loves, that his employees love, that he doesn't have to pay to maintain, and that makes his employees want to stay.

Small Business Owner Using the IGIC as a Business Cash Account—The Ultimate Golden Handcuffs

Regina Holden owns and runs a successful trial law firm. She has three attorneys, six paralegals, a file clerk, and a receptionist on staff. She has always paid her employees generously and provided full medical benefits, but she has never been able to stomach the thought of paying the costs of a 401(k) just to put her employees into what she knows is a bad plan.

Regina already has multiple IGICs for herself, the cash value of which she used to build her business and continues to use for that purpose. It will also serve as her eventual retirement account. She earns enough money to pay for an additional account, but she has already purchased the maximum amount of death benefit she can for herself: $21 million.

Regina wants to create more IGIC accounts but can't insure herself for anymore. Because she has been using an IGIC for several years, she knows the basics. After consulting with an IGIC expert, she decides to set up an IGIC account for some of her employees to use to grow her business. This is what she does:

1. Regina tells her attorneys and paralegal employees that she is going to set up a life insurance contract for each of them. She then set each one up for a different amount based on how much she valued that individual employee. Her law firm was the owner of the insurance account, but the employees were the insureds. They all got to pick their respective beneficiaries for themselves.

2. Regina tells the employees that their accounts come with a cash value that belongs to and can be used by the law firm. The death benefit is a tax-free benefit to the employees' heirs.

3. Regina makes the employees aware that after five years, half the value of the cash value will be theirs, and after ten years, the entire value of the cash value will be theirs, plus whatever else the law firm contributed for as long as they remained employed.

4. During the first five years of an employee's IGIC, Regina will borrow against the cash account to fund her case costs, pay for marketing, recruiting, and otherwise grow her business. The money inside the cash account will continue to grow even as she grows it outside the account.

5. During the second five years of an employee's IGIC, the employee will now have access to half the cash to borrow against for the employee's own investments, expenses, etc. Regina will continue to use the other half in combination with the other employees' IGICs to fund her business.

6. After ten years, the plan has fully vested (which is really just based on the contract between Regina and the employee and not any sort of formal or government-related vesting). The employee gets the entire cash account, giving them a healthy start to their retirement, plus a good amount of cash they can use for their own purposes.

7. If an employee leaves the firm before the cash value has vested, they forfeit the cash value that isn't theirs.[14] Regina is going to continue to pay that former employee's premiums so that she can take advantage of the benefits of the account for the rest of the employee's life (benefits she has already maxed out for herself). This is a huge boon to the employee, too. No matter what the employee does in the future, as long as Regina keeps paying those premiums (and it is in her best interest to do so), the employee's family has a guaranteed death benefit when the employee dies—just because they once worked for Regina.

By setting up her business this way, Regina is able to upsurge the amount of cash value she can use for her business and provide a very strong disincentive for her employees to leave—all they have to do is look at the cash in that account and see what they'd be giving up. It would have to be a pretty compelling offer to walk away from it.

---

14. Regina will likely buy them out to prevent complications of ownership with future contributions and growth. Alternatively, she can just set the terms differently at the beginning so that it is all forfeited if the employee leaves before ten years. Or to almost anything she wants.

With a 401(k), we believe the money is ours, even though we have almost none of the rights of property ownership associated with it.[15] In the meantime, others are making money off of our money. When we reach age 59½ (or whatever age the government changes it to), we can start using the money for ourselves if we want, paying taxes on anything we use.

Using the IGIC, there is no pretending the money belongs to the employee. The employee knows that it is only theirs if they meet the minimum requirements for obtaining it: in this case, remaining employed for a minimum period. In the meantime, the employer is using the money to grow the business. From the employee's perspective, at least during the vesting period, it feels a lot like a 401(k), except all the terms are disclosed and known to the employee. If it vests, they're a lot better off—all without having contributed any of their own money.

But even if her employees do leave, and the program never vests, both parties are still better off for the relationship. Regina gets to keep the cash account, keep contributing to it, and use it however she wants; and the employee gets to keep the death benefit no matter where they go.

Small Business Owner Getting More Bang for Her Buck with an IGIC Account

Geri Miller owns a growing commercial construction company that does a lot of work in the Southwest United States. Her operating expenses exceed $100,000 per month. Her company, Miller Construction, sponsors a 401(k) plan where she does a 100 percent match for her forty-five full-time employees. The average match per employee per year is around $4,000, but the company will match up to $5,000 per year per employee. (Not all of these employees take advantage of the full match.)

In addition to the $180,000 ($4,000 x 45 employees) that Miller Construction contributes to the 401(k) plans, it spends about $65,000 per year

---

15. See discussion beginning on page 37.

just in costs associated with the plans. Miller gets to deduct the $180,000 in contributions, but much of the $65,000 in costs are not tax deductible.

It also spends about $30,000 per year in costs associated with employee turnover, including paying for recruitment and training.

That's when Geri learned about the IGIC as a 401(k) alternative. She doesn't have to get rid of her 401(k) plan to participate, but once she educates herself, she wants to. This is what her company does:

1. Miller Construction stops contributing to 401(k) plans and terminates them. It tells its employees it is going to set up an IGIC-based plan instead. It gives the employees the option of rolling into the IGIC or converting their 401(k) into an IRA. There is a cost associated with the rollover, including state-mandated filing fees for the entities required to do it, but it is well worth the benefit.

2. Because the IGIC plan has no maintenance costs, Miller Construction has now freed up $65,000 per year that it can use for any other legitimate purpose. For example, to reward its best employees, Miller Construction can decide to use those freed-up funds to create larger IGICs for them. Because the IGIC is not subject to anti-discrimination testing, it can choose which employees to reward.[16] Or it could choose not to contribute to other employees. So Miller Construction, not the U.S. Government, gets to choose what it believes is fair. Alternatively, it could use those funds to create an IGIC for Geri herself, and it will be like having a free retirement account just for switching from the 401(k).

3. By creating incentives to stay, Miller Construction has also significantly reduced employee turnover, which means it is spending less in turnover costs.

---

16. Miller Construction cannot discriminate based on age, race, gender, or any other protected class, but it can recognize the value of rewarding hard work and loyalty (i.e. discriminate based on merit).

Miller Construction is still spending the same amount of money, but now more of it is going to what Miller Construction wants to spend it on. The employees are much better off because they're no longer investing in the government taxation-during-retirement plan.

These are just three examples of potential scenarios for the employer. The employer can set this up in an infinite number of ways. The one constant is that there are no set-up[17] or annual maintenance costs, so all the money that goes into the plan actually goes into the plan. And then of course, it comes with all the advantages an IGIC has over a qualified plan. It's a win-win-win.

---

17. There are no set-up fees to create this plan, but there are government-related costs associated with converting a qualified plan to an IGIC.

CHAPTER 22

THE POWER OF LEVERAGING

"Banking is very good business if you don't do anything dumb."
— WARREN BUFFETT

THE USE OF CASH VALUE INSURANCE has always been associated with the term "banking." Sales concepts like "Infinite Banking," "Be Your Own Bank," "Banking on Yourself," and "Family Banking" all capitalize on the fact that when you have cash value life insurance, you can, in a sense, become a bank.

Instead of going to a bank for a loan, you can use your accumulated cash value to make a loan to yourself. And then instead of paying interest to the bank, the interest goes to you. You're earning interest inside your insurance contract on the cash value, but you're also earning outside the contract in the interest you pay yourself (or on investment gains). Thus, like a bank, you are using the same money more than once.

These concepts have caught on for good reason: no one wants to be beholden to a bank, but we'd all love to be the bank. But these concepts also fall short because the power of banking doesn't come from using the same money twice, but using it over and over and over again.

How Banks Make Money

The lifeblood of a bank is new deposits. Because banks make money charging interest on loans, the more money they have on deposit, the more they can make on loans. The Federal Reserve System requires banks to have at least 10 percent of their total deposits on reserve (meaning held by the bank), while the other 90 percent can be used in loans.[1]

---

1. Board of Governors of the Federal Reserve System, "Reserve Requirements," federalreserve. gov, March 15, 2020, last accessed July 9, 2020, https://www.federalreserve.gov/monetarypolicy/reservereq.htm.

UN$HACKLED

If you deposit one hundred dollars in a savings account, the bank will pay you a contracted rate of interest, but then the bank can then turn around and use ninety dollars of that toward a loan to someone else. The bank will charge interest on that loan and earn money on your money. The national average interest rate on a personal loan is 9.41 percent.[2] If you bank at Wells Fargo, Bank of America, Chase, or U.S. Bank, you'll earn 0.1 percent interest annually on the balance of your savings account.[3]

That seems like a pretty good deal for the bank, right? Without using their own money and just for giving you the privilege of holding your money with them, they'll earn 9.41 percent on your ninety dollars while paying you 0.1 percent on one hundred dollars. After a year, they've earned $8.47 and paid you ten cents. So they're up $8.37. That's pretty much an infinite return on their investment because they invested zero dollars (remember, they're using your money, not theirs) and experienced a net return of $8.37.

If you could earn $8.37 for every zero dollars invested, how many times would you invest zero dollars? As many times as you could, right?

Well, because of our fractional reserve banking system, it gets even better than that for the bank because they can, in a way, create money out of thin air and then make money on that money.

When the bank lent out ninety dollars of your deposit, someone else now has ninety dollars they didn't have before in the form of a loan. Perhaps they took it as part of a car loan. So they take that ninety dollars they got from you, and in combination with money from 90 percent of other people's deposits, they go purchase a car.

The seller of the car now has new money, which she deposits into her bank. Included in that deposit is your ninety dollars. Suppose that the seller banks at

---

2. Brianna McGurran, "What's a Good Personal Loan Interest Rate," Experian, January 27, 2020, last accessed July 9, 2020, https://www.experian.com/blogs/ask-experian/whats-a-good-interest-rate-for-a-personal-loan.
3. Matthew Goldbert, "Average Savings Interest Rates for 2020," Bankrate, May 5, 2020, last accessed July 9, 2020, https://www.bankrate.com/banking/savings/average-savings-interest-rates.

the same place you do.[4] Now that bank—your bank—has another ninety dollars in new deposits. The bank probably doesn't know (and certainly doesn't care) that ninety dollars of the deposit can be traced back to your hundred-dollar deposit.

Now, according to the bank's records, you have one hundred dollars in your account, and the seller of the vehicle has ninety dollars (amidst the rest of the deposit) in her account. It now appears that there is $190 in the economy, even though there is really only one hundred dollars—your hundred dollars. So how does that affect you? In most cases, it doesn't at all.

After you deposited your hundred dollars, and the bank lent out ninety dollars, how much money did you have in your account? You still have a hundred dollars, don't you? If you wanted to go withdraw a hundred dollars, even though the bank only had ten dollars of it, you could still do so, right? Absolutely.

To fulfill your request, the bank is going to take the ten dollars it kept on reserve from your deposit and pair it with ninety dollars from its 10 percent reserves of other people's money. Everything will be just fine as long as everyone with an account doesn't go to take out all their money at the same time. In other words, banks only work as long as we are confident they will work.

A scene from the unforgettable *It's a Wonderful Life* captures well the concept of faith in banking. The citizens of Bedford Falls lose confidence in George Bailey's bank, Bailey Bros. Building & Loan Association, after one of its loans is called due early. There is a panicked bank run, where everyone seeks to withdraw their money because they fear it won't be there later if they don't. Jimmy Stewart, playing George Bailey, tries to explain why they can't all have their money at once:

> No, but you . . . you . . . you're thinking of this place all wrong. As if I had the money back in a safe. The money's not here. Your money's in Joe's house . . . [to one of the men] . . . right next to yours. And in the Kennedy house, and Mrs. Macklin's house, and a hundred others.

---

4. Even if she banks elsewhere, the other bank is going to receive the new deposits and extend up to 90% in loans, and your bank will just get deposits from others. A rising tide lifts all boats.

Why, you're lending them the money to build, and then they're going to pay it back to you as best they can. Now what are you going to do? Foreclose on them?[5]

So let's assume that all is well with your bank. From your original one-hundred-dollar deposit, it now has $190 on the books, all of which can be drawn against by the respective account holders (you for one hundred dollars and the seller of the vehicle for ninety) as long as it doesn't happen all at once.

Because the bank now has another ninety dollars in new deposits, the rules say it must keep 10 percent on reserve (nine dollars) and it can lend out the rest (eighty-one dollars). And so the cycle continues. Because the mandated reserve rate is 10 percent, the bank can make loans ten times with the same money, shrinking incrementally by 90 percent with each generation of loans.[6]

If we take that out ten generations and assume the bank always loans at the full 90 percent allowed, charging 9.41 percent for each new loan and paying you 0.1 percent annual interest, this is what your one hundred dollars does for the bank after one year compared to what it does for you after one year:

Step	$ Deposited	$ Reserved	$ Lent	Bank Growth	Depositor Growth
1	$100.00	$ 10.00	$90.00	$8.47	$0.10
2	$90.00	$9.00	$81.00	$7.62	$0.09
3	$81.00	$8.10	$72.90	$6.86	$0.08
4	$72.90	$7.29	$65.61	$6.17	$0.07
5	$65.61	$6.56	$59.05	$5.56	$0.07
6	$59.05	$5.90	$53.14	$5.00	$0.06

---

5. *It's a Wonderful Life* © 1946.
6. Prateek Agarwal, "Money Multiplier," Intelligent Economist, July 1, 2019, last accessed July 9, 2020, https://www.intelligenteconomist.com/money-multiplier.

Step	$ Deposited	$ Reserved	$ Lent	Bank Growth	Depositor Growth
7	$53.14	$5.31	$47.83	$4.50	$0.05
8	$47.83	$4.78	$43.05	$4.05	$0.05
9	$43.05	$4.30	$38.74	$3.65	$0.04
10	$38.74	$3.87	$34.87	$3.28	$0.04
Total	$651.32	$65.13	$586.19	$55.16	$0.65

Your single one-hundred-dollar deposit introduced $651.32 in new money into the bank's ledgers. The bank, in turn, took $586.19 of that and wrapped it into loans that produced a total of $55.16 in interest growth in one year. Then, in turn, it had to give sixty-five cents of that profit to its depositors over the same year, one dime of which went to you for your one-hundred-dollar deposit, and the other fifty-five cents went to the other depositors. The bank's net gain was $54.51, which is a 54.51 percent return on investment of the original one hundred dollars that was not the bank's to begin with.

That seems like a really good deal. Why aren't more of us doing this? Well, today's your lucky day.

Leveraging Your IGIC Like a Bank

Now that you have a clearer understanding about how banks make money, perhaps you have come to the same realization I have: if a bank can use the same money ten times, but I can only use the same money twice in an IGIC (once to grow in the insurance contract and once to borrow against to use it outside the insurance contract), that doesn't seem very much like banking at all.

If that was your realization, then you are keener than you look because you're spot on. But what if I could show you a way you could leverage your cash value not just once or twice, but up to ten times or more?

Let's say you have $100,000 in a bank account. Maybe it represents years' worth of savings. Maybe it was from a recent inheritance. You know that the hundred dollars you'll earn in interest over the next year is too low to justify leaving it there. You have read the first twenty-one chapters of this book and think you want to stick it in an IGIC.

Of course, you can do that. But because of the MEC guidelines introduced by the legislature in the 1980s, you can't just put in all of your premium of an insurance contract in a single year. You have to have premium going in one or more subsequent years for it to qualify as an insurance contract.[7] If you want to use the IGIC to invest tax free or pay off debt, that's probably exactly what you would have to do. But suppose you just wanted to invest your money and maximize the growth—you don't need access to it immediately and just want it to jump-start your retirement savings.

What we're going to do is set up an insurance contract that will allow you to put in $100,000 every year.[8] Then you are going to use your $100,000 cash to pay the first year's premium.

Fast forward eleven months. You are one month away from your premium becoming due. You go to a bank, and you say something like this: "Bank, I have $100,000 in cash value life insurance. I would like to use that as collateral for a $100,000 loan."

Even if you've never been rejected for a loan, you've seen enough movies where banks cruelly deny a loan to know that getting a loan isn't always easy. Collateral and creditworthiness become very important because a bank makes loans based on measured risk.

---

7. There are ways to create a single-premium policy, but those won't have the other attributes you're looking for in a policy.
8. When we do this, we have to be mindful of your maximum insurability. Based on your age and income, you only qualify for a certain amount of death benefit, which in most cases is in the millions. There will also only be a certain amount of annual premium you can contribute based on your income. For most, the limits are far outside what they want to incorporate into their plan, but with the leveraging plan, because the benefits are so huge and the cost so low, those limits often become the delimiting factor of an investment plan.

Banks are willing to loan on real estate in the form of a mortgage because the risk is relatively low. Even if you default, the loan is secured by the real estate itself. Since real estate typically increases in value and always stays in the same place, the bank is confident that if the borrower defaults on the loan, it will not only be able to find the property to foreclose on it, but it will likely have enough equity (between interim increases in value and your monthly payment) to repay the balance of the loan.

There is still some risk, though. Property values don't always rise, either because of market fluctuations or owner neglect. If the bank does have to foreclose, it has to hire an attorney and go through a lengthy and often expensive statutory foreclosure process. Foreclosure costs balloon even further if the homeowner files for bankruptcy.

Banks also are usually comfortable lending on a vehicle purchase. Even if the vehicle doesn't retain its value like a home does, measures in place like auto insurance and gap coverage give banks an added dose of reassurance. Even so, if the borrower defaults and the bank has to repossess, it has to hire a repo man and take steps to track down the vehicle.

Perhaps the single safest collateral that can form the basis of a bank loan is cash value life insurance. By giving the bank a lien on your cash value, the bank knows there is always easy-to-find, easy-to-access security on its loan. Banks recognize the creditworthiness of the mutual insurance company and know that in a whole life policy, the cash value is guaranteed to grow. If they ever do need to call in the note, they don't have to track down the collateral or hire an attorney, private investigator, or repo man to collect. In the next chapter, we discuss why banks invest billions of dollars in life insurance.[9] Put simply, it's because these loans are so secure.

So when you go to that bank and ask for a $100,000 bank loan and are willing to put up $100,000 in cash value life insurance as collateral, you're going to get that loan. Because it's such a safe loan, there are banks willing to give it to you for as low as 2 percent net simple annual interest.

---

9. See discussion beginning on page 231.

So now you are two weeks before your second $100,000 premium is due. You've got $100,000 loaned cash in your checking account. You are going to use that money to pay your second-year premium.

The insurance contract now reflects $200,000 worth of premiums working on your behalf.

At month eleven of year two, you're going to go to the bank again. This time you're going to say, "Bank, I have $200,000 in cash value life insurance. Half of it is already pledged to you for a prior loan. I would like to take the other half, $100,000, and use it as collateral for a new $100,000 loan." Just like last time, the bank is going to give it to you, and once again, you're going to use it to pay your next year's premium. And you're going to do that again every year.

Fast forward ten years. You have now paid one million dollars in premium—the original $100,000 in cash and another $900,000 you've borrowed from the bank.

Over the last ten years, those premiums have been working for you. Each of them is growing based on the guaranteed interest rate and the nonguaranteed dividend.

Let's look at the growth in just year ten, assuming a 5 percent interest-plus-dividend rate.

You've got a million dollars in principal working for you (we'll ignore the interest and dividends on the last ten years of growth for now). At 5 percent growth, your account will increase by $50,000.

Remember, you only ever used $100,000 of your money. But in year ten alone, you've got an increase of $50,000, which is a 50 percent return on investment in one year!

But you also have interest accruing against you. In year ten, you have $900,000 in loans that are accruing interest at 2 percent annually. In year ten alone, you have $18,000 in interest accruing against you. Your net gain in this scenario is $32,000, a 32 percent gain. Still, not too shabby. And this growth is all tax free.

What about that loan? In some cases, the banks will not require monthly payments and will just collect the balance from the death benefit when you die. In other cases, your IGIC will be making regular interest-only payments with the balance being paid off by the death benefit. But in either case, it's the plan itself that pays the interest. You never have to come up with new money to pay interest or principal.

Let's fast forward to year twenty. You have still only put in $100,000 of your own money, and the bank has contributed $1.9 million. So you have $2 million growing at a rate of 5 percent in year twenty, and you have $1.9 million growing against you at a rate of 2 percent in year twenty. In that year alone, you are up $100,000 on the growth, down $38,000 on the interest, with a net gain of $62,000, which represents total net growth in that year of 62 percent!

Now let's take into account the fact that your growth is compounding. In year twenty, you don't just have $2 million working for you. You also have twenty years of prior growth added to that balance. So in reality, year twenty's balance will be more than $3 million, representing an average, year-over-year return of about 19 percent on your original $100,000.

That's a pretty good boon to a tax-free retirement. At that point, not only are you enjoying being unshackled yourself, but you are probably going to be dancing a jig and running around unshackling your friends and neighbors with your newfound wisdom and freedom.

CHAPTER 23

WHAT'S THE CATCH?

"Diligence is the mother of good luck."

– BENJAMIN FRANKLIN

IF YOU ARE LIKE A LOT OF PEOPLE I have spoken to over the years, you may be thinking this sounds too good to be true or wondering what the catch is. Let's spend some time on this. I would hate for you to pass on a wonderful opportunity just because it sounded really good.

First, I would never suggest anyone use their money for anything without first doing their own due diligence. There are a lot of scammers out there. Some of them are deliberately trying to scam you. In fact, as I have been sitting here writing, I received an email from someone soliciting my services as a lawyer. The email was written in broken English, has a link it wanted me to follow, and everyone in my office received the exact same email. It didn't take long for us to conclude that we weren't going to click on the link or respond.

Perhaps more dangerous are those who, like some financial planners and CPAs, believe they are giving you sound advice but just don't know what they don't know.

For several years, I taught paralegals at UNLV (University of Nevada, Las Vegas). One of the skills I tried to instill in them was the value of being able to discern truth from error in online research. They were encouraged to do independent research beyond the supplied course materials. The hard part is not finding information (there are terabytes of it out there); it's figuring out which information is valid. Some of the paralegals quickly discovered that even relying on the attorneys they worked for was not always smart.

That's going to be particularly difficult if what you are researching falls outside the bounds of conventional wisdom. Nevertheless, reputable sources are out there if you are patient and determined enough to find them.

227

UN$HACKLED

To help you in your due diligence, let me explain to you some of the limitations and drawbacks of the IGIC.

YOU STILL HAVE TO PAY SOME TAXES WITH THE IGIC

We have emphasized the tax advantages of an insurance contract—which manifest themselves most strongly when you invest and during retirement. But that's not to say you're getting out of paying your taxes. The government will always get its due.

Remember, like a Roth IRA—which allows you to invest tax free and is not taxed during retirement—the IGIC is funded using *after-tax* dollars.[1] So every dollar you use to fund your IGIC premiums is a dollar that was never part of a tax deduction and is yours after you've paid your taxes.

The balance of your IGIC is not taxed during retirement only if you're willing to leave the cash value growth in the account and borrow against it.

Then when you die, the cash value reverts back to the insurance company (they have to pay taxes on their profits like any other business), and the death benefit goes to your heirs. The death benefit, which was never the main purpose of your IGIC, is going to be less than it would have been otherwise because it doesn't go to your heirs until after it repays any balance on your loan.

So in the final analysis, it isn't that IGIC facilitates tax evasion—it's just a measured choice to pay taxes now at a known rate on a known amount rather than later on an unknown sum at an unknown rate for an unknown timeframe. Taxes in some form are inevitable. Take your medicine and never look back.

---

1. When you use a qualified rollover, this is the exception. But in that case, your taxes become due but not until your required minimum distributions are due.

THE IGIC'S GUARANTEES ONLY APPLY TO MONEY INSIDE THE POLICY

When you park your investment fund with a mutual insurance company, you are placing your money in about the safest place it can be. There are competitive, guaranteed rates of return, plus nonguaranteed dividends.

But if you're going to use the IGIC to its full potential, you're going to want to invest *outside* the contract, too. The IGIC cannot guarantee against loss outside the policy. You could borrow against your policy, invest in real estate, and then discover that the home you purchase is full of mold, resulting in almost a total loss on your investment. You could invest in cryptocurrency only to have the bottom fall out. You could invest in mutual funds right as the market is about to correct and find yourself waiting several years for it to recover.

The IGIC does not eliminate risk. For outside investments, you still have to be smart and do your due diligence.

NOT EVERYONE QUALIFIES FOR AN IGIC

Although we like the IGIC as an investment vehicle, to maintain its tax-preferred status, it still has to meet the definition of life insurance under 26 U.S.C. 7702. You still have to be insuring a life.

And because the actuaries at the insurance company measure risk to make sure when the insurance company invests in you, it is a good investment, your age and health become very important factors.

If you are too advanced in age (it gets harder to insure someone once they're in their 70s), you might not be insurable. In fact, the younger you are, the better rates of return you're going to experience. If you have significant health problems that could potentially increase your mortality (history of cancer, obesity, heart condition, etc.), you may either be uninsurable or have to pay more for the cost of insurance. The more you pay for insurance, the less benefit you get from the cash value, though usually the difference is marginal.

Additionally, there is a limit to how much life insurance you can get. The more money you make, the more insurance you can get—the death benefit was designed to be a replacement of lifetime income, after all. That means there are upper limits to what you can put into one of these accounts.

However, those upper limits are very high. They are far higher than what you can put in a qualified account, and in many cases, high enough that those investing don't have enough money to put in it for that to even be a factor. But for some, the limits do restrict what they can put into the plan.

We can do several things to get around some of these roadblocks—insuring a spouse or child, for example. There is still a lot we can do within the law and the parameters insurance companies set. Unfortunately, though, not everyone who wants an IGIC will be able to get one.

WHAT IF THE INSURANCE COMPANY GOES UNDER?

In these days when banks and other financial juggernauts—multibillion-dollar companies like Merrill Lynch, Lehman Brothers, and Bear Stearns—can fail, it is only natural to question the long-term viability of any company acting as a custodian for your money.

But there is a huge difference between a bank that overleverages itself and a mutual life insurance company—owned by those who own policies. Mutual insurance companies have the track record and longevity they have (many of them having been around for almost 200 years) precisely because they are conservative. These are companies with A+ or A++ credit ratings—ratings given based on independent assessments of their financial strength.

But even assuming the worst—that the company holding your policy fails—there are safeguards in place.

For one, remember that insurance companies are private for-profit entities. Every insurance policy they have is an asset. That's how they make money. Sears recently closed its doors. One of its exclusive brands, Craftsman, was an asset. Even though Sears went under, Craftsman still had value, so Black and Decker bought it (for $900 million), and you can now find it on the shelves of Lowe's.[2]

It is the same with mutual insurance companies. The insurance contracts have value. Although very few mutual insurance companies have ever failed, those that have were smaller, more localized companies. When that happens, one of two things occurs: Usually a company that is more financially sound will purchase them. If not, then a guaranty association or third-party will administer the policies, which continue in force and are funded by a state fund designed to insure against insurance loss.[3]

As evidence of just how safe these investments are, consider this: banks, like all other businesses, exist to make money, except the service they provide is handling your money. They give you a safe place to hold your money, make it convenient for you to spend your money (checks and debit cards), charge you here and there for the privilege (ATM withdrawal fees, overdraft charges, and monthly charges if you don't maintain a minimum balance), but they make most of their profits taking the money you entrust with them and investing it through mortgages, student loans, car loans, etc.

That's not the only investment they're making. In fact, banks put billions (yep, that's billions with a "B") of dollars into whole life insurance contracts like investment grade insurance contracts. Because banks are federally regulated and

---

2. Chris Isidore, "Sears' Iconic Craftsman Tools Coming to Rival Lowe's," October 21, 2017, last accessed July 9, 2020, https://money.cnn.com/2017/10/24/news/companies/craftsman-lowes-sears/index.html.

3. National Organization of Life & Health Insurance Guaranty Associations, "Mutual Benefit Life Insurance Company," last accessed May 21, 2020, https://www.nolhga.com/companies/public/main.cfm/NAICCode/66362/GAID/100.

insured through the Federal Deposit Insurance Corporation (FDIC), and the FDIC is a federal agency, banks are required to disclose their financials.

If we look at the balance sheet for the four biggest banks in the United States, which separates their holdings into asset classes, we can see how much bank-owned life insurance each of these banks owns compared to one other asset (real estate):

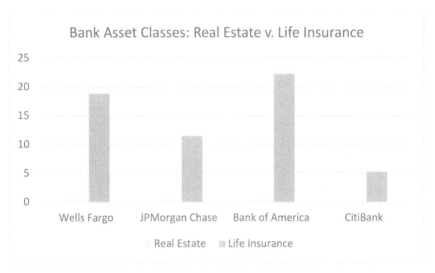

Bank Asset Classes: Real Estate v. Life Insurance

Numbers are in billions of dollars. Real estate investments (not including the buildings the banks are occupying) are on the left. Bank-owned life insurance is on the right. Figures are from the June 2019 report.[4]

You might have to squint to see the real estate lines on the graph. Because what banks invest in real estate—which many investment gurus will tell you is the safest and best investment[5]—is just a sliver in comparison to what they're investing in cash value life insurance.

---

4. To look up banks on your own, go to the FDIC's website's institution search at https://www7.fdic. gov/idasp/advSearchLanding.asp. Enter the name of the bank you want to look up under "Institution Name," and click "search," which is a blue button underneath. This will give you a list of banks. Click on the Cert number highlighted in blue to the left of the name of the bank you searched. Then click on the "Generate Report" button in the baby-blue bar on the right side. There it is.
5. I'm not knocking real estate. It really is and can be a great investment if done right, especially if it is purchased using a tax-free investment vehicle, like the IGIC, as a basis.

Why is it that these four banks alone have almost $60,000,000,000 ($60 billion) in bank-owned life insurance? Because banks understand how money works. And they understand cash value life insurance.

When it is said mutual insurance companies are about the safest place to park your money, there is good reason.

CHANGING LAWS

One big question I am frequently asked is something like this: "How do you know that Congress will not change the tax laws to eliminate the IGIC as a viable tax-free investment vehicle?"

That's a very good question. One of the lessons you've hopefully learned from this book is that Congress can and does change the rules all the time. It certainly is possible that Congress changes something to take away what might be the last great investment vehicle. They've got a lot of deficit to make up, after all, and have to get it from somewhere.

Although I can't guarantee that will never happen, I don't think it will. For one thing, we have been through this more than once. On one such occasion, in 1985, the Treasury Department proposed changes to the tax code that would strip cash value life insurance of its tax-advantaged status. On the official record, during the 1985 session of Congress, we find some colorful language in this regard from one citizen who offered testimony to Congress in opposition to the Treasury Department's attempt to eliminate some of the tax benefits associated with cash value life insurance:

> The Treasury Department on life insurance with the Congress is like [a small insistent child]. Congress has told the Department "No, No," and after almost two years of pleading last year, "No" again! Well, here they are again, and I'm afraid. Why? Because I really don't think Congress is going to pass a new tax on people's

life insurance, and I don't think the Treasury Department thinks so either. But, I can sure see them exhuming the corpses of their oft repeated proposals buried again by Congress last year. I am afraid of them encouraging the Congress to reintroduce those proposals at some stage of the legislative process. I can hear them now, whispering at mark-up, "Let the insurance industry have tax-free inside build-up, but reduce the income tax basis of the policy by the "Economic Benefit" value of the equivalent yearly renewable term premiums, as we proposed in 1983; and severely limit the tax deductibility of policy loans, as we proposed in 1983 and '84 and '85; and treat policy loans in excess of basis as taxable distributions, like we did to annuities in 1984. Let's make a "compromise" with the insurance industry and ask them to give up something in return for the tax-free unrealized appreciation of life insurance policy living cash surrender values."Our new model for 1985."

*   *   *

The Great Lady of Life Insurance would suffer sudden death at the hands of a new tax on the unrealized appreciation of all policies; or the slow death of a new tax on the unrealized appreciation of new policies; or be permanently financially disfigured by the acid of non-deductibility of interest (current proposals); and/or taxing the proceeds of policy loans; and/or reduction in the income tax basis of the policy by the imputed equivalent yearly renewable term insur‑ ance premiums (previous Treasury proposals).[6]

If you can believe it, Congress actually defended tax treatment of insur‑ ance contracts. An entire host of congressional legislators from coast to coast added its voice to the chorus of opposition:[7]

- Senator Jeremish Denton (Alabama) to Treasury Secretary Baker: "I am writing you to urge that Treasury amend its tax reform proposal to eliminate those provisions that would affect the taxation of life insur‑ ance companies and their policy holders. I believe that enacting those provisions would be both unfair and unwise."

- Senator Alphonse D'Amato (New York): "I assure you that I will be watch‑ ing carefully to see if the provisions impacting life insurance are removed."

- Senator Paula Hawkins (Florida): "A provision that I find objection‑ able is the proposed taxation of the inside interest build-up in life insurance policies and annuities. This cash build-up makes adequate life insurance affordable throughout one's lifetime. Since cash values are not realized income, this provision would essentially be creating a tax on cash that is not received annually and would discourage tax payers from purchasing permanent policies."

6. United States Congress, House, Committee on Ways and Means, "Comprehensive Tax Reform, Hearings Before the Committee on Ways and Means, House of Representatives, Ninety-ninth Congress, First Session, on the President's Tax Proposals to the congress for Fairness, Growth, and Simplicity, May 30; June 4, 5, 7, 11, 12, 13, 14, 17, 20, 25, 26, 27; July 8, 9, 10, 11, 12, 17, 19, 22, 25, 26, 29, 30, and 31, 1985," at 6613, last accessed May 21, 2020, https:// play.google.com/books/reader?id=GQaIMnWs6a8C&hl=en&pg=GBS.PA5857. To find this exact page, follow the link, which will take you to a digital facsimile of the entire record. At the bottom of the screen is a scroll bar, and you are looking for page 757 out of 1168. This will take you to page 6613 of the record.
7. All of these excerpts were taken from the same congressional record referenced in footnote 6 of this chapter starting on page 6614 of the record (which is 758/1168 of the scroll bar at the bottom).

UN$HACKLED

- Representative Philip Crane (Illinois): "The increased taxation of insurance policies, and even the taxation of interest received from savings accounts, only discourages the savings and investment necessary to spur on economic growth."

- Senator Don Nickles (Oklahoma): "Taxing the 'inside buildup' or increased cash value of a policy is not a reform of an existing tax; it is a brand new tax. The plan would base this new tax on a benefit not received and would be complex to report and administer. As a result, most policyholders would surrender the policy to pay or to avoid the tax. For life insurance policy loans, the Treasury proposed to tax those loans as distributions. These loans are simply that, a loan to the policyholder from his accrued benefit in the policy. He will repay that loan with interest or it will be deducted from the death benefit.... Loans of any kind should not be taxed. Another negative impact on policy loans is the proposal to limit the deductibility of nonmortgage interest. This would have the effect of reducing life insurance in force thereby eliminating needed capital to stimulate the economy."

- Representative Howard Coble (North Carolina): "The original proposal from the Department of the Treasury calls for the taxation of the 'inside buildup' of life insurance policies. The results of this would be catastrophic. Not only would this destroy any incentive for savings within the insurance industry, but it would have a negative impact on the Treasury in the long run. This change would remove the incentive to purchase permanent life insurance protection and would therefore generate tremendous lapses of policies, encouraging individuals to buy term insurance. As I am sure you are aware, term insurance becomes extremely expensive as an individual grows older and, in all likelihood, will be terminated before death. In other words, there will be many widows without benefits who will be relying on the federal government to care for them in the future."

- Senator John Heinz (Pennsylvania): "The financial security of many Americans who rely upon life insurance policies could be severely affected by this Treasury proposal. Because of the taxing of the inside buildup, individuals may be unwilling or unable to purchase the life insurance they feel they need for protection. This taxation also might cause policyholders to abandon permanent cash value insurance in favor of term policies, which do not provide the dependability and certainty of permanent life insurance."

- Representative Michael Andrews (Texas): "Treasury's current proposal would treat the owners of life insurance as having actually received the cash value which has accumulated during the past year and, therefore, tax this value as income even though policyholder access to 'cash value' is generally in the form of a loan which they must repay with interest."

- Representative Bud Shuster (Pennsylvania): "Taxing the annual increased value of life insurance is tantamount to taxing the interest on certificates of deposit although the interest is not received until the certificate matures."

- Representative Doug Walgren (Pennsylvania): "Taxing the increase in cash values of life insurance policies is especially troublesome to me, since we have always adopted the approach that income should not be taxed until it is realized."

- Representative Bart Gordon (Tennessee): "I promise to oppose legislation which unfairly singles out one segment of our society. For this reason I am against the proposed taxation on 'inside buildup' of permanent life insurance policies."

- Senator Edward Zorinsky (Nebraska): "Many have written to me opposing the taxes that, in effect, would be imposed on ... the cash buildup of life insurance. Let me assure that I oppose these changes in the law."

- Senator Russell Long (Louisiana): "I certainly agree that life insurance serves important social purposes in our society, and that we must keep those purposes in mind when we consider tax and other legislation. In this connection, in 1984 I opposed the addition of policyholder restrictions to the Life Insurance Tax Act. In particular, I and my Senate colleagues were successful in eliminating the House-passed provision that would have singled out policy loan interest for restrictive tax treatment."

- Senator Bob Packwood (Oregon): "As you know, I have been quite active in maintaining the incentives for employee benefits. I am also aware of the potential problems that taxing the buildup of cash values of life insurance and removing the deductibility of loan interest would present to policyholders."

- Representative Judd Gregg (New Hampshire): "I would not support the taxation of the inside buildup on insurance policies."

- Representative Nancy Johnson (Connecticut): "This tax proposal, in addition, would put insurance beyond the reach of those who need it most. Families struggling to make ends meet would find this added tax burden unacceptable and would forego the valuable protection insurance provides. As the Treasury proposal is a radically new concept and actually taxes 'phantom' income—money that the policy holder is unable to use or invest elsewhere—I will oppose it."

- Senator Orrin Hatch (Utah): "Under present law, the policyholder is not taxed on increases in the cash value unless the contract is surrendered prior to the death of the insured for an amount in excess of the gross premiums paid. Since Congress has recently studied this issue in depth and made extensive changes in the Internal Revenue Code, it would not be in our best interest to again consider further changes in policy."

- Representative Robert Smith (New Hampshire): "I commend the life insurance industry for this cash solvency and I realize how detrimental the taxing of a policy's cash or loan value would be. This is not tax simplification but a blatant discriminatory tax against the insurance industry and is unfair to the individuals who have invested in these insurance programs for personal or family security."
- Representative Matthew Rinaldo (New Jersey): "The increase in the cash value of life insurance policies could increase the taxable income of many families and discourage investment in essential life insurance protection."
- Representative Mike Synar (Oklahoma): "Americans buy whole-life insurance to protect their families and other beneficiaries in the event of death. A tax on the annual increase in cash value—which the insured collects only if the policy is surrendered—would increase the cost of this essential component of a family's financial plan. I reject the argument that term life insurance is an alternative."

Why do you suppose members of Congress were so quick to defend the tax advantages of cash value life insurance? If I had to guess, it's because of the tax benefits they themselves enjoy from using these investment vehicles.[8] For example, in these debates about whether to strip life insurance of some of its tax advantages, one representative shared, "I oppose taxing the accumulated cash value of an insurance policy; I am all for savings incentives and believe insurance has been a savings vehicle. I personally borrowed against my insurance when I had children in college."[9]

8. All members of Congress must disclose their financials, and they are publicly available. However, although you can see what they're investing in, they do not have to disclose their investment vehicle.
9. Sam Gibbons (Florida). United States Congress, House, Committee on Ways and Means, "Comprehensive Tax Reform, etc." https://play.google.com/books/reader?id=GQaIMnWs6a8 C&hl=en&pg=GBS.PA5857 at 6610 (754/1168 of the digital pagination).

As one member of the House of Representatives noted, employing logic uncharacteristic of Congress:

It has been reported that the nation's largest corporations revealed they paid no income tax, 165 of them. Included in this was General Electric, which earned $6.5 billion of income, and not only paid no tax, but received a $293,000 refund. Assuming the proposed 20 percent alternative minimum tax for corporations would be applicable to this income, the new revenue you raised from General Electric alone would be $600 million more than by taxing every life insurance policy owner and annuity owner ....

As one opponent of the changes pointed out—the changes would not be growth productive because they wouldn't actually increase tax revenue:

The 200 million of projected revenue ... from the taxation of permanent cash value life insurance will never happen. The Treasury Department always makes a fundamental error in their assumptions in projecting tax revenue that the economic activity of the nation is going to stay the same. Assuming that people will continue to buy level premium permanent living cash value life insurance burdened by these onerous new taxes, is equivalent to assuming that the number of people going to the beaches will remain the same regardless of the number of sharks in the water. Plain, old fashioned, common horse sense dictates that nobody will buy policies which create a tax cost in addition to non-deductible premiums. If no premiums are sold, no new tax is created. "Where's the beef?"

Congress ultimately did not make the proposed changes and did not strip life insurance of its tax-favored status. They may have found this argument, presented to them in opposition of the changes, persuasive: "[In addition to Disneyland, which was financed using a loan Walt Disney took against the cash value of his life insurance,] Thousands of small businesses across this nation have been saved, started or grown because of the utilization of the loan values of permanent living cash value life insurance on the life of the business owner."[10]

They did, however create the definition of life insurance that prevented the use of life insurance to shelter huge sums of money in cash value without a comparable death benefit. But even then, those who had high cash value insurance contracts before the change were grandfathered in. This new rule, the MEC rule, applies only to those contracts entered into on or after June 21, 1988.[11]

For any future changes to the tax code that may affect insurance contracts, we expect the same to be true—first, that members of Congress will defend the last great investment vehicle, and second, that any changes they do make will not apply retroactively.

But what about the states? Every state has the opportunity to tax its citizens, so what if they seek to impair your use of an insurance contract? State law already differs as to the asset-protected status of the cash value and death benefit, as well as a surviving spouse's right to a death benefit even if not named as beneficiary. Could a state try to change the tax status of an insurance contract? Thankfully, the answer is almost definitely "no."

Every statutory amendment—every congressional change—must pass constitutional muster. This means it is held up against the protections afforded by the U.S. Constitution, and if there are any inconsistencies or contradictions, the Constitution wins.

One of those protections is found in the Supremacy Clause, which says that to the extent the federal government has a law covering a certain topic, no state can implement a law that contradicts it.[12] In other words, it would be very

10. *Id.*
11. 26 U.S.C. § 7702A(a)(1)(A).
12. U.S. Const. Art. 6 cl. 2.

difficult for a state lawmaking body to create tax laws specific to life insurance policies, which are governed and covered by 26 U.S.C. 7702.

Fortunately for us, there is also something in the Constitution called the Contracts Clause, which also applies specifically to states: "No state shall ... pass any ... Law impairing the Obligation of Contracts ..."[13] The legislature of any state is prohibited from enacting any law that retroactively impairs contract rights.

The threshold inquiry in an application of the Contract Clause is "whether the state law has, in fact, operated as a substantial impairment of a contractual relationship."[14] Where the legislation nullifies an express term of the contract that was bargained for and reasonably relied upon by the parties, resulting in a completely unexpected liability, the Contracts Clause renders it unenforceable.[15]

Total destruction of contractual expectations is not necessary for a finding of substantial impairment.[16] If the state regulation constitutes a substantial impairment, the state must have a significant and legitimate public purpose behind the legislation,[17] such as the remedying of a broad and general social or economic problem.[18]

What that means in layman's terms is that if you have a pre-existing contract, like an insurance contract, and the contract is enforceable as written and complies with then-current state law, the state can't pass a law that retroactively and substantially impairs those contract rights unless it has a really good reason.

Is it possible that the life insurance contract, the last great investment vehicle, is destroyed with the stroke of a Congressional pen? Yes. But it is highly unlikely. Even if it does happen, those who already have insurance contracts will be locked in and exempt. Immune from future shackling, you could say.

---

13. U.S. Const. Art. I § 10 cl. 1.
14. *Allied Structural Steel Co. v. Spannaus*, 438 U.S. 234, 244, 98 S.Ct. 2716, 2722 (1978).
15. *Id.*
16. *United States Trust Co. v. New Jersey*, 431 U.S. 1, 26–27, 97 S.Ct. 1505, 1519–20 (1977).
17. *Id.* at 22, 97 S. Ct. at 1517.
18. *Allied Structural Steel Co.*, 438 U.S. at 249, 98 S. Ct. at 2723–25.

CONCLUSION

"The key to success is to start before you're ready."
— Marie Forleo

FOR MOST OF US, we think of money as linear. We work, we earn money, it goes into our account, and then we either spend it immediately, or we save/invest it, and then spend it later. Money is to be earned and spent, sometimes being saved or invested for a period between being earned and spent.

Further, while we are thinking linearly, we also recognize that at some point on that timeline, between when we make the money and when we spend it (and sometimes even after), the government levies taxes. We are taxed when we earn it, when we save it, when we invest it, when we retire, when we die, and then our heirs are taxed on money passed on to them.

Indeed, although Benjamin Franklin created a pithy phrase[1] when in a letter to a friend, he wrote, "In this world nothing can be said to be certain, except death and taxes,"[2] he could not have imagined that this one phrase would fashion countless generations' ideas about taxes.

The truth is, there is nothing certain about taxes. The tax code is constantly changing in unpredictable ways. The best way to insulate yourself from those changes—which you can't control—is to insulate yourself from future

---

1. He wasn't actually the originator of this phrase, but he's the most famous person to have said it. Two published sources before him with variations of the phrase include Christopher Bullock, *The Cobler of Preston* (1716) ("'Tis impossible to be sure of anything but Death and Taxes,") and Edward Ward, *The Dancing Devils* (1724) ("Death and Taxes, they are certain.").
2. Benjamin Franklin, letter to Jean-Baptiste Le Roy, November 13, 1789.

changes by meeting your tax obligations now, when they're known and can be planned for.

It is an unfortunate reality of capitalism that those who offer you a product or service tend to highlight the benefits without mentioning the drawbacks. Of course, when you were first introduced to qualified plans, no one asked you, "Would you rather put your money over there where you can pay off the government's debts, or would you rather put it over here where you can use it?" If they had, there wouldn't have been much of a choice at all.

But now you have that choice. Whether you're starting out or you have a growing nest egg to roll over, it's not too late to cast off the chains of conventional wisdom and become the master of your own future—unshackled.

FURTHER INFORMATION

IF AFTER READING THIS BOOK, you realize you would like further information or legal or financial advice related to your circumstances and would like to speak to me or a member of my financial team, please feel free to reach out to us.

I own and operate a law firm called the Fortune Law Firm. We are based in Las Vegas, Nevada, but do business with people nationwide. You can look us up at fortunefirm.com and find out a little more about us there. You can also call us toll-free by dialing 833-400-4999 or email us at contactus@fortunefirm.com.

If the person who answers the phone does not make your day better by at least putting a smile on your face, let me know. We take smiling very seriously around here.

ACKNOWLEDGMENTS

MY FIRST GREAT TUTOR IN MONEY was my lovely wife, Amber. She came to the marriage debt free and responsible. I came with student loans and a motorcycle. It was an uphill battle, but she helped shape me into who I am today.

I could not have created this book without the tutelage of tax expert Nick Fortune, who taught me much of what I know about taxes and money and who is an integral part of what I do now.

I would be remiss also if I did not express gratitude for Angela Malis, who helped shape our business into what it is now. She is really good at what she does.

Many thanks to John Highland, whose confidence in my writing and high-level connections led to the conversations necessary for publication.

Thank you to Michelle Borquez-Robinson, whose cheery expertise made it possible (and enjoyable) to get this book off the ground.

As with any endeavor worth doing, it can't be done alone, and this book would certainly have been different (read: inferior) without the expert mind and work of my editor, Sherrie Clark. She had the patience to hear my diatribes on grammar and the grace to run with it. Emily Hitchcock and her design team deserve high praise for an aesthetic and readable inside copy. They also get the credit for the beautiful typography on the cover.

For better or for worse, a book's cover is one of it's most important elements, and this book's cover wouldn't be what it is if my brother, Jacob Parry, had not had the courage to tell me I could do better, which took us back to the focus groups and the drawing board. His uncompromising skill and vision took the book to the next level with his cover design.

A hearty thanks to Stephanie McReynolds for the enthusiasm and gusto with which she took to my ideas for an unconventional book launch party. Although a combination of factors, including Covid-related shutdowns, made the launch impossible, I know it would have been epic.

Connie Wetzel, thank you for your endurance and expert advice during our audiobook recording sessions. Without you, the book would have been unlistenable. With your feedback and coaching, I sound way better than I am. It made all the difference.

A big heartfelt thanks to Jamie Bridges and A Room with a View Studios for your hospitality during recording and for splicing me together to make it sound like I read the entire book without stuttering, coughing, or tripping over my own words.

And thank you to you, the reader, for caring about my ideas. Words on a printed page are just useless shapes of ink until a reader gives them meaning.

ABOUT THE AUTHOR

ZACH EARNED HIS LAW DEGREE from the University of Illinois, graduating magna cum laude, and has since taught several university-level law courses and published over fifty legal articles and a book currently used as the text for a legal course at University of Nevada, Las Vegas.

For over a decade, Zach was a civil litigator and trial attorney who was able to win several multimillion-dollar judgments, expose the vulnerabilities of business entities, engage in veil piercing to destroy the corporate shield that litigants thought protected them, and find creative and diverse means to effectuate collection. As a first-chair trial attorney, he never lost. He is undefeated on appeal.

He also gained experience in administrative disputes, including with the Financial Industry Regulatory Authority (FINRA), which gave him a unique insight into the inner workings of the financial planning industry.

Along the way, Zach learned some unexpected lessons about how money works: how to earn it, grow it smarter, and keep more of it.

While thriving as a trial attorney, Zach partnered up with a tax expert and started a second law firm, the Fortune Law Firm,[1] which was dedicated to helping clients with tax planning, investments, and retirement. Zach has since sold his trial practice to dedicate his efforts to the Fortune Law Firm, where he currently works with his clients to create a comprehensive tax and asset protection plan to help them keep more of what they earn.

---

1. Fortune Law Firm, 11920 Southern Highlands Parkway, Suite 200, Las Vegas, Nevada 89141, 833-400-4999, contactus@fortunefirm.com, https://fortunefirm.com.